FIGHTING THE GOOD FIGHT

FIGHTING THE GOOD FIGHT

A Brief History of the
Orthodox Presbyterian Church

D. G. Hart and John Muether

The Committee on Christian Education and
The Committee for the Historian of the
Orthodox Presbyterian Church
Philadelphia ◆ 1995

The title of this book comes from the apostle Paul, whose words in I Timothy 6:12 provided the text for J. Gresham Machen's final sermon at Princeton Theological Seminary, delivered March 10, 1929. Machen's message was entitled "The Good Fight of Faith" and continues in print in the Banner of Truth publication God Transcendent, a collection of Machen's sermons.

Cover Photo: The Eleventh General Assembly of the Orthodox Presbyterian Church met at Westminster Theological Seminary, Philadelphia, May 16–19, 1944. Those attending the assembly gathered for this picture on the porch in the garden outside Machen Hall. The moderator of the assembly was Edwin H. Rian, and Edward Heerema served as stated clerk.

Library of Congress Cataloging-in-Publication Data

Hart, D. G., and Muether, John
FIGHTING THE GOOD FIGHT: A BRIEF HISTORY OF THE ORTHODOX
PRESBYTERIAN CHURCH
    1. Church History—Presbyterianism
    2. American Denominations—The Orthodox Presbyterian Church
    I. Title   II. Presbyterian Church
ISBN 0-934688-81-8

Book designed and typeset by Eric D. Bristley
Olive Tree Communications
Set in Goudy Old Style
Printed in the United States of America

To the first generation of the
Orthodox Presbyterian Church,
which sacrificed much to fight the good fight of faith

Contents

Preface

MEMBERS of the Orthodox Presbyterian Church and many interested in this expression of the visible body of Christ have waited years for the production of a more thorough treatment of OP history. As far back as the 1960s, a call was heard in the general assembly for something to be done—and not without reason, since nearly everything written to that point concentrated on the church's formative years.

Since the sixties, the church has established the historian's position and celebrated its fiftieth anniversary. Beginnings were made by the historian, not unconnected to that celebration, to gain a more comprehensive picture of the church's life and significance.

What has become clear from these efforts, at least to this writer and the authors of this book, is that the OPC's identity is bound to her origins. In other words, the OPC was born a certain type of church. This means her identity is not tied so much to her collective self-understanding as it is to her existence as such. She has an assigned identity, one that is Reformed to its very soul, one that the church denies to her detriment and loss.

The OPC, by the grace of God, stands out as a remarkable chapter in the chronicle of church history. She is a statement against the insidious drift of mainline Protestantism, a challenge to an often misdirected and theologically weak evangelicalism, and a clear rejoinder to fundamentalism. She has been a positive, although not always consistent, testimony for Presbyterianism in the orthodox Calvinistic sense.

The authors of this book understand these things and are especially well-suited to write a history of the OPC. They know the church—John Muether because he was raised in it, and has loved and studied it; Darryl Hart because he chose it after a long journey through seminary and graduate school that included the detailed investigation of J. Gresham Machen's life and OPC beginnings. Here is sound assessment—to be sure, not without evaluation and criticism as in all historical writing; but a valuable reading of the OPC's story meant for the church's edification, the communication of the truth, and the glory of the triune God of the Bible.

This book has been written to accompany the 1993 video which provides a visual history of the OPC (see the list of recommended sources for study of the OPC, p. 211). As in the case of the video, the book has been produced by both the Committee for the Historian and the Committee on Christian Education. It was reviewed prior to publication by six readers: James Alexander, F. Kingsley Elder, James S. Gidley, Brian O'Leary, David K. Thompson, and myself. Lawrence R. Eyres, Robert W. Eckardt, and Arthur W. Kuschke, all ministers who have lived through the OPC's history, also read the manuscript and offered helpful critiques. Kathleen Bristley served as copy editor and proofreader. Eric Bristley designed the book.

Not everyone agreed with every detail or opinion in the text; nor will every reader. However, those most directly responsible for the book speak in highest terms about its intention and content and pray that it will be most useful to you in the interests of the "good fight" (1 Timothy 6:12).

Charles G. Dennison,
Historian for the Orthodox Presbyterian Church
May 15, 1995

Introduction
The History and Identity
of the OPC

THE ORTHODOX PRESBYTERIAN CHURCH is the heir of a marvelous heritage. Its theological and ecclesiastical roots are grounded in the dramatic struggles and remarkable accomplishments of the Protestant Reformation. Among the stalwart forefathers of the OPC are such names as John Calvin, the reformer who established a beachhead for the Reformed faith in Geneva, John Knox, the feisty Scottish churchman who followed Calvin's insights to begin Presbyterianism, and Ulrich Zwingli, the first-generation reformer in Zurich who elaborated many of the truths which to this day the Reformed community continues to hold dear.

The genius of the Reformation was its recovery of the biblical faith of Christ alone, grace alone, the Bible alone, and faith alone. While the reformers of the sixteenth century made significant contributions to the cause of the Reformed faith, the OPC owes a special debt to the British theologians and pastors who assembled during the 1640s to draft the Westminster Confession of Faith and Catechisms. For the Westminster Standards not only have become the theological touchstone for the OPC, but in the estimate of many Presbyterians the confession and catechisms embody the fullest and clearest exposition of the insights of Calvin, Knox, and Zwingli. According to Benjamin Warfield, one of the greatest Presbyterian theologians in the history of the United States, the Westminster Standards "mark an epoch in the history of human reflection on the truths of the gospel—an epoch in the attainment and registry of doctrinal truth." For this reason J. Gresham

3

Machen, a central figure in the founding of the OPC, could claim that the Reformed faith, "the creed God has taught us in his Word," was "glorious." The OPC, to the extent that it continues to uphold this magnificent line of Christian truth, is indeed a grand church.

Yet the OPC is not the only Presbyterian or Reformed church whose origins can be traced to the Reformation. There are, in fact, fourteen different Presbyterian denominations in North America, including the mainline Presbyterian Church in the USA, the Presbyterian Church in America, the Associate Reformed Presbyterian Church, the Reformed Presbyterian Church of North America, and the Korean Presbyterian Church. So what makes the OPC different from these other Presbyterian bodies?

Spokesmen and apologists for the denomination have offered different answers to this question. For Richard B. Gaffin, Jr., professor of systematic theology at Westminster Theological Seminary in Philadelphia, the basic identity of the OPC is what binds it together with "all churches built upon the foundation of the apostles and prophets with Jesus Christ himself as the chief cornerstone." According to John P. Galbraith, a man with many years of service in the OPC, the denomination is grounded in the belief "that God's Word is Truth," and that "the Westminster Confession of Faith and Catechisms interpret that Truth most truly." In *The Presbyterian Conflict*, a book that chronicled the events that led up to the founding of the OPC in 1936, Edwin H. Rian wrote that the OPC "is what its name implies, truly Presbyterian. . . . It is a church devoted to the Bible as the final authority for faith and practice and convinced that only through the sacrificial death of Christ upon the cross can men be saved."

This little book, a brief history of the OPC designed for use in adult education classes and church study groups, is written from the perspective that one of the things that makes the OPC different from other churches is its history. The authors believe that a proper understanding of the OPC must include some knowledge of the denomination's past. The church's history reflects the unique emphases and particular concerns of Orthodox Presbyterians.

We also want to claim a bit more for the history of the OPC in the pages that follow. Many Americans show little interest in history. Henry Ford spoke for many when he said, "History is bunk." Then, of course, there is the common American notion, perhaps the result of declining high school standards, that history is just one endless and boring series of names, dates, and political treaties. Since Presbyterians value highly the accomplishments of the Reformers and look to the confessions and creeds of the six-teenth and seventeenth centuries for sustenance and guidance, they tend to be more interested in the past than the average Amer-ican. But even Presbyterians do not always see the immediate val-ue of studying history.

For this reason we are convinced that the value of studying the OPC's history lies in the close connection between the church's past and the church's identity. In recent years theologians and ed-ucators have explored the ties between narrative and identity. The argument has been made that stories shape the identity of a people. From the plays of the Greeks to the family stories that parents tell their children, narratives powerfully nurture a sense of purpose and allegiance which is crucial to the way a people understand them-selves and their relationships to others.

This observation about the importance of narrative is not merely an anthropological truism but appears to correspond to bib-lical teaching. A common refrain heard in the Old Testament is God commanding the Israelites to tell their children the wonder-ful stories of the exodus when God delivered his people from the bondage of Egypt. These narratives lay at the heart of what it meant to be part of God's people. Similarly, in the New Testament the Gospels recount the narrative of God's delivering his people from bondage to sin in the death and resurrection of Jesus Christ. At the same time, the epistles stress the importance of those events, of "Christ and him crucified," for the identity and faithful-ness of the early church. In this sense Christians are a people de-fined by stories just as much as are immigrant groups in the United States who describe themselves by the heroic accomplishments of previous generations.

To carry this analogy further, to be Presbyterian is to tell and live out the gospel narratives in a particular way—not just one way, but the truest and best way. But within the Presbyterian fold there are a variety of differences which separate the diverse de-nominations, just as within the realm of people who speak English there are differences of idiom, accent, and slang. To put this another way, all Presbyterians subscribe to the Westminster Confession of Faith and Catechisms, but the different Presbyterian denominations subscribe to these theological standards in divergent ways. These differences in subscription can be compared to various ways of following the rules of grammar for a particular language. Some English speakers have been sticklers over the niceties of grammar, while others prefer slang and care little for grammatical precision and correctness.

This analogy between the variety of Presbyterian churches and linguistic differences among English-speakers should not be read in any way as an approval of relativism. For we hold that just as there are rules of English grammar which determine proper usage, so there is a correct way of expressing and practicing the Reformed faith. Thus, while all Presbyterians speak the same theological language, we believe the OPC uses the correct language, the King's English as it were. This book can be read as both the story which gives the OPC its identity and in turn as a primer in Orthodox Presbyterian grammar. For the OPC, though imperfect in many ways, has throughout its short history tried to tell and live out the story of the gospel of Jesus Christ faithfully. In many instances in the life of the OPC, subjects have not always agreed with verbs, words have been misspelled, and vulgarisms have crept in. But the church has also distinguished itself for trying to remove these errors and above all for endeavoring to be faithful to God as he has revealed himself in his Word as summarized in the Westminster Standards.

For this reason, if the OPC is to figure out its identity, it needs to understand its roots. Here a comparison between the OPC and the experience of immigrants in the United States may be helpful. Typically, the first generation of immigrants pays much attention to and takes its identity from the strenuous and courageous efforts which established the group in a foreign land. And this was very much the case with the founding generation of the OPC, who retold frequently the events that led to the founding of the denomination. Second-generation immigrants, however, are less interested in the accomplishments of the past and more concerned to assimilate to the host society. This pattern also seems to be true of the OPC. Second-generation Orthodox Presbyterians have manifested a concern to reach out beyond the confines of the OPC to the wider evangelical community. But just as third-generation immigrants often turn back to recover the achievements of the first generation, so the OPC, as it matures to the stage of a third generation, stands poised to reconsider and recover the accomplishments of the denomination's founders. We hope this book will be used to stimulate such an interest, for we believe the history of the church holds the key to the denomination's identity. To that end we also hope that readers will not stop with this small volume but will also work through the suggestions for further reading at the end of this book.

It should be stated at the outset that the authors write with specific convictions or biases (depending on your perspective) about Reformed faith and practice generally, and about the OPC specifically. We acknowledge that our perspective is not shared by all in the denomination. This book is not intended to silence other perspectives but to contribute to a healthy discussion of the OPC's identity and mission. We hope it will persuade the unpersuaded, confirm the already committed, and prompt those who disagree to voice disagreement. Above all, we hope that this book will challenge the church to think hard about its identity. For we believe that a church without an identity will lose its reason for existence.

One theme that stands out in the pages that follow is controversy, hence the title, *Fighting the Good Fight*. And this theme is prominent for a good reason. The debates, struggles, and inner turmoil that have hounded the OPC have been a vital part of the denomination's history and identity. The OPC was born in the midst of the fundamentalist-modernist controversy and it has continued to experience disputes and strife throughout its history. In fact, the OPC has a reputation for not backing away from controversy. This record of conflict reflects in part the church's commitment to follow God's Word faithfully, a commitment that will always involve opposition to sin and error and will often generate conflict. As Dr. Machen said, "The gospel of Christ, in a world of sin and doubt will cause disputing; and if it does not cause disputing and arouse bitter opposition, that is a fairly sure sign that it is not being faithfully proclaimed." Machen's recognition that controversy "of the right sort" is inherent in Christianity reflects the biblical truth that the Christian life is one of constant warfare against sinfulness and disobedience. Just as individual believers this side of glory will al-

ways be prone to sin because of their old nature, so the visible
church always has to struggle against disobedience. The OPC has
understood this truth, and its history reflects a vigilant effort to be
on guard against departures from God's Word. While some may regard this tendency of the OPC as a blemish, we see the church's
effort to eliminate error both as a virtue and as a characteristic
which distinguishes the church from other Protestant communions. And, in this regard, we believe that the OPC has been especially attentive to the apostle Paul's injunction to Timothy to
"fight the good fight of faith" (I Tim 6:12).

Finally, some mention should be made about the general tone
of the narrative that follows. Rather than chronicling the OPC's
past in glowing and jubilant rhetoric, we have chosen an approach
that is best described as understated. Some readers may be frustrated by this choice. Like those who focus exclusively upon the
mighty deeds of the Protestant Reformation, some may want to
hear only about the success and triumphs of the OPC. But good
history should be faithful to reality, and the OPC, over the course
of its history, has achieved nothing like a worldly splendor. For
that reason it is difficult to write the history of the OPC as one of
extraordinary achievements. Like it or not, the stormy and modest
past of the OPC does not on the surface compare well with the
magnificent accomplishments of the Protestant Reformation. This
is indeed frustrating and humbling, especially when we believe we
have the truth and want that truth to be reflected in a significant
and influential manner. Nevertheless, the OPC has not produced
presidents of the United States, it does not have a record of establishing megachurches, and it has no institution of higher learning.
Other Presbyterian denominations may be able to point to accomplishments like these. The OPC cannot.

Nevertheless, we believe the subdued history which follows is
entirely appropriate. For the denomination is best compared to a
small but nevertheless firm presence in American Christianity—
easily overlooked, but when confronted not easily ignored. As historian Mark Noll, who compared the OPC to the "pea beneath the
mattress," said at the celebration of the church's fiftieth anniversary, the denomination "is very small, but it is rock hard and unde-
niably *there*." While some might want to think of the OPC as a
jewel of great price hidden away by the forces of darkness, Noll

cautioned that Balaam's ass may make for a better comparison. The denomination "has not sold its soul to theological fashion or to the allure of wealth, power, and influence." Rather, "like Balaam's ass, though a thing of naught and the humblest of all God's creatures, it has seen the angel of God and tried to heed his word."

As insignificant as the OPC may appear and as uninspiring as its history may seem to some, the church's past turns out to convey an important Christian truth. The Bible makes clear that God has not often used the mighty and powerful to achieve his ends. Israel was always a minor player in the annals of ancient near eastern history, and the apostles were by no means powerful or famous. In fact, God's people have often been poor, common, and humble. As the apostle Paul wrote, God uses "jars of clay to show that this all-surpassing power is from God and not from us" (II Cor 4:7).

This is not to say that the OPC should celebrate its inferiority or take its cultural marginality for granted. But this is a reminder that suffering, humility, and adversity characterize God's people. So if the OPC has not produced celebrities or if its methods have not been followed by the rest of the Protestant world, it does not mean that God has not blessed the church in less visible or celebrated ways. God's people have a different measure for success and influence than the world's standards. According to Paul, "we fix our eyes not on what is seen, but on what is unseen. For what is seen is temporary, but what is unseen is eternal" (II Cor 4:18). We believe that this insight is what motivated the OPC at its founding, sustained it at critical periods in the denomination's development, and will be crucial to the church's faithfulness now and in the next century. And we trust that the pages which follow will establish and confirm this truth within the minds and hearts of Orthodox Presbyterians, not for the sake of their denomination's importance, but, as the first question and answer of the Westminster Shorter Catechism puts it, for the glory and enjoying of God.

PART ONE
ORIGINS

IN 1927, only two years after the infamous Scopes Trial in Dayton, Tennessee, where the popular Presbyterian layman and prominent Democrat politician, William Jennings Bryan, had prosecuted the case against teaching evolution in public schools, J. Gresham Machen was asked to become the president of Bryan Memorial University, an institution commemorating the Christian statesman's accomplishments. Machen refused the offer. He was so busy with controversies both in the Presbyterian Church and at Princeton Seminary that a move to a new school would have compromised his usefulness to conservative efforts against theological liberalism in Presbyterian circles.

Time magazine actually reported on the invitation to Machen, an indication of Bryan's continuing notoriety and the publicity surrounding the Scopes Trial and the fundamentalist controversy. For this reason it was no surprise that Machen's refusal would eventually be published in *Moody Monthly*. More curious, however, was the substance of his reasons for declining the position. Machen wrote to the board of trustees,

> I never call myself a "Fundamentalist." There is indeed, no inherent objection to the term; and if the disjunction is between "Fundamentalism" and "Modernism," then I am willing to call myself a Fundamentalist of the most pronounced type. But after all, what I prefer to call myself is not a "Fundamentalist" but a "Calvinist"—that is, an adherent of the Reformed Faith. As such I regard myself as standing in the great central current of the Church's life—the current which flows down from the Word of God through Augustine and Calvin, and which has found noteworthy expression in America in the great tradition represented by Charles Hodge and Benjamin Breckinridge Warfield and the other representatives of the "Princeton School."

What is noteworthy about these remarks is Machen's self-conscious identification not just with the Reformed faith, but also with the particular tradition represented by the theologians and churchmen at Princeton Seminary. Most of Machen's contemporaries thought of him as a fundamentalist, pure and simple. But he thought of himself as part of something that was both broader and narrower than interdenominational fundamentalism, namely, the noble theological tradition stretching from the apostle Paul to the great theological insights of the Westminster Assembly and the distinctive beliefs and practices of American Presbyterianism.

Many people since Machen's time have been hard pressed to distinguish a fundamentalist from an Orthodox Presbyterian. Both came to life during the 1920s and 1930s, both have been judged narrow and intolerant, and both hold to a faith that is at odds with the way most modern men and women live and think about their lives. But, while the ecclesiastical struggles that led in 1936 to the founding of the Orthodox Presbyterian Church were part of the culture wars that came to be known as the fundamentalist-modernist controversy, Machen's purposes as a leader of the new denomination, demonstrated in the quotation above, were remarkably different from mainstream fundamentalism. Just as there are differences between political conservatives, like the ones separating those who favor free markets from others who stress issues of public morality, so there are differences between the conservatism of fundamentalists and Orthodox Presbyterians. Whereas fundamentalists looked back to the American traditions of revivalism and moral crusades to abolish slavery and alcohol, Machen took sustenance from the theology and practice of true American Presbyterians like Hodge and Warfield, the leaders of what was called "Old School Presbyterianism."

The following chapters cover the Presbyterian controversies which involved Machen in the struggles against liberalism and led to the founding of the OPC, as well as the initial conflicts within the new denomination which stamped its early identity. They demonstrate that the OPC was established not just to oppose the theological liberalism which had infected America's mainline Protestant bodies, but also to preserve and champion older Presbyterian habits and convictions. These chapters also show that in order to understand the OPC we need to look be-

yond the issues raised by fundamentalists in the 1920s to the concerns that have throughout American history informed the
tradition of confessional Presbyterianism.

1
J. Gresham Machen and the Crisis of Presbyterian Identity

IN THE SPRING OF 1920 as J. Gresham Machen, then a relatively unknown professor of New Testament at Princeton Seminary, made plans for service at his first general assembly of the Presbyterian Church in the USA, he was still adjusting to the routines of "normalcy" in post-war America. Only nine months earlier he had returned from France where he had witnessed the atrocities of World War I while working as a secretary for the YMCA. But even though Machen enjoyed leaving behind the hardships of life at the front—the poor sleeping conditions, the bad food, the constant threat of attack, and above all, the destruction of human life—his desire for normalcy did not prevent him from gearing up for one of the greatest battles in the history of American Christianity, one which would begin at the Assembly of 1920 and would only be complete with the founding of the Orthodox Presbyterian Church sixteen years later.

The commissioners to the general assembly were to deliberate and vote on a proposal that would have dramatically compromised the witness of the Northern Presbyterian Church which Machen actively served. J. Ross Stevenson, the President of Princeton Theological Seminary and well-respected leader in Presbyterian affairs, reported on a plan to unite the nation's largest Protestant denominations into a national federated church. "The Philadelphia Plan," as it was called, was designed to coordinate and consolidate the activities of eighteen different denominations. In some cases this would mean the merger of several small churches in rural towns into a larger "union" congregation. In all cases it meant the

sacrifice of theological integrity because the plan called upon denominations to put aside doctrinal distinctives for the purpose of
achieving greater influence and relevance. And while the plan in-
voked the biblical imperative that Christ's disciples be one,
Machen, along with other conservative Presbyterians, opposed the
initiative as a subtle form of error masquerading as scriptural truth.

From Machen's perspective, the unity of the church could
never be isolated from the truths to which Christ had called his
people to witness. The creedal basis of the plan, he wrote in one of
three articles designed to defeat the proposed union, omitted the
"great essentials of the Christian faith." Most disquieting was a
paragraph in its introduction which relegated the Westminster
Confession of Faith to nothing more than a denominational affair.
This view of the confession implied that there was virtually no difference between Presbyterians, Baptists, Congregationalists, Lutherans, or other Protestant bodies. Even more insidious was the idea
that what united Christians was religious experience and that theology was merely a manifestation of Christians living at different
times and in diverse places. For those who believed that the Confession of Faith was the system of truth revealed in Scripture,
Machen concluded, such a basis for church union would always
produce the fiercest opposition.

Within a few years the Philadelphia Plan was defeated. But
the controversy that erupted at the 1920 General Assembly revealed widespread ambivalence within the church and the denomination's seminaries about the central convictions of Presbyterian
faith and practice. The controversy about church union became,
in effect, a prelude to the conflict over Protestant liberalism. For
the tendency to sacrifice theological teachings for more effective
witness, which characterized the plan for union, was also central
to the logic of theological liberalism. And the strongest opponents
of church union, many of whom were ministers and elders from the
Philadelphia vicinity, would also emerge as the leading critics of
Protestant liberalism. In both cases, in the debates about church
union and throughout the fundamentalist controversy, Presbyterian theology and practice were at stake. Thus, instead of returning
home to a quiet life of scholarship and preaching, Machen came
back from a Europe ravaged by war only to face an enemy even

more dangerous than the Kaiser's army, one which would not kill the body but could destroy the soul.

What is Presbyterianism?

The word "Presbyterian" is derived from the Greek word *presbyteros* (meaning *elder*), and it refers to a particular form of church government. But historically, Presbyterianism entails more than that. In addition to polity, Presbyterians have certain convictions about the doctrine and worship of the church. These three elements—polity, doctrine, and worship—are reflected in the ordination vows of the OPC. Among those vows, candidates for church office are asked to "receive and adopt" the Westminster Confession of Faith "as containing the system of doctrine taught in the Holy Scriptures," and they are asked to "approve of the government, discipline, and worship of the Orthodox Presbyterian Church." And it was the theology of the Westminster Confession that Machen believed was under attack during the 1920s by ministers and denominational executives of the Presbyterian Church.

As we have suggested, "Presbyterian" has come to mean more than a form of church government. With other heirs of the Protestant Reformation, Presbyterians have historically held a high view of the authority of Scripture. The Westminster Confession states that the Bible is the Word of God and is our "only rule for faith and obedience." It was a departure from that high view of Scripture and a substitution of the word of man for the Word of God in the Presbyterian Church during the fundamentalist controversy that led to the exodus from that body and to the formation of the OPC.

Presbyterians are also Calvinists: they affirm the "Reformed faith." The Reformed faith is sometimes summarized as the "five points of Calvinism"—total depravity, unconditional election, limited atonement, irresistible grace, and perseverance of the saints. These five points are helpful ways of understanding the sovereignty of God in our salvation. It is through grace alone that we are saved: salvation is found only in the electing love of God, the substitutionary atonement of Jesus Christ, and the application of Christ's work through the work of the Holy Spirit.

But the Reformed faith is more than that. It affirms the sovereignty of God in all of life. It is a way of life that seeks as its main purpose "to glorify God and to enjoy him forever." The clearest summary of the system of doctrine is found in the Westminster Confession of Faith, together with its Larger and Shorter Catechisms. And so the Orthodox Presbyterian Church, while holding the Bible as its only infallible rule of faith and practice, has adopted the Westminster Confession and Catechisms as its subordinate standards.

Reformed theology as expressed in the Westminster Confession also relies upon the idea of the covenant. The confession explains that the Bible has one central message: God's salvation of his people through Jesus Christ. The entire Bible is about God's covenant of grace with his people. Covenant theology refuses to divide the Bible into different dispensations with different ways of salvation. From beginning to end the covenant of grace is the story of salvation by grace. The covenant unfolds from its establishment in the garden of Eden to our present age, the period between Christ's ascension and second coming. The Old Testament prophesies about the coming of Christ, and the New Testament describes and explains his coming.

The doctrine of the covenant shapes the life of God's church in important ways. Covenant theology does not regard the church as a group of individuals who voluntarily join a religious club but as a household of faith that God has graciously chosen and sustained as his people, the body of Christ through the fellowship of the Spirit. All of God's people are uniquely gifted for service in his kingdom with special offices instituted by Christ for the ministry of worship, nurture, and evangelism. Thus, no Christian is an island. Participation in the work of the church, both through supporting and submitting to it, is essential to walking in the way of the covenant.

Furthermore, covenant theology refuses to distill the Bible into a set of fundamentals or spiritual laws. Since all Scripture is God-breathed, the "whole counsel of God" is to be preached, and the sovereignty of God impacts all of life.

Finally, as we shall explore in a later chapter, the covenant affects our attitude toward our children. They are a heritage of the Lord. We baptize our children because they belong to God. The covenantal promises of God extend to believers and their children.

History of Presbyterianism

Presbyterians have not been unanimous in their understanding of Calvinist theology, however. This has meant that throughout the history of Reformed and Presbyterian churches, conflict and division have regrettably taken place.

Modern Presbyterianism traces its origin to the giants of the Reformation such as John Calvin and John Knox. These reformers saw the restoration of both theology and church order as essential to their purpose. Jesus Christ, not the pope, is the only mediator between God and man and thus the only ruler of his church. He rules his church directly through his Word and Spirit.

English-speaking Presbyterianism began with the Scottish preacher John Knox. Knox fled to Geneva in exile in 1555, and there he formed a congregation modeled on Calvin's teaching about government, confession, and worship. He returned to Scotland in 1559, helping to establish the Presbyterian church there by drafting the Scots Confession and the Book of Discipline. Presbyterianism came to the New World in two waves, first with the early Puritan settlements, and later with the Scotch-Irish immigration in the seventeenth century. Colonial presbyteries were organized in the early eighteenth century, and the Presbyterian Church in the USA was established in 1789 with its first general assembly.

Because of the denominational controversies of the twentieth century, it is tempting to imagine that American Presbyterianism before the twentieth century was orthodox. The truth is that doctrinal controversies constantly confronted the church. From the earliest days of American Presbyterianism there were disagreements over the degree to which the church would adhere to its confessional standards. These disputes were usually described as debates over subscription, that is, how strictly must Presbyterian ministers subscribe to the Westminster Confession? Throughout the early history of the Presbyterian Church, the sides were divided into "loose subscriptionists" and "strict subscriptionists." The former consisted of New England Puritans influenced by revivalism who, it seemed to others, stressed personal piety at the expense of doctrinal precision. The Scotch-Irish ministers, on the other hand, tended to be more confessionally oriented and bound by church order.

The tension between the pietistic and confessional groups divided the church into "New Side" and "Old Side" camps during the Great Awakening of the 1740s. The New Siders gained popular support through the revival preaching of men like George Whitefield and Gilbert Tennent. Their emphasis on the holiness of God and the sinfulness of men and women convicted thousands of hearers and revived Calvinistic orthodoxy in colonial America. Yet Old Siders feared that the excesses of revivalist psychology were a threat to Presbyterian order and theology. While revivals reached many with the gospel, they also undermined the authority and order of the local congregation and pastor. Revivalism made the individual's experience central to Christian faith and practice, thus downplaying the importance of word, sacrament, and the communal character of membership in Christ's body.*

Split in 1741, the two sides were united again in 1758. But tensions between revivalism and confessionalism were to emerge again with the Second Great Awakening in the early nineteenth century. The revivals of this period, like those before American independence, demonstrated commendable zeal for reaching the lost and prompted many heroic efforts to reform society. But the Second Awakening, different in some ways from its predecessor, stressed the individual's decision for Christ, even to the point of attacking Calvinism as elitist and the ministry as antithetical to democratic individualism. Evangelists like the Presbyterian Charles Finney employed "new measures," techniques of revivalism copied from Methodists which appeared to make grace dependent upon human initiative. Some Presbyterians left the church

---

* It should be noted that we distinguish here between revivalism centered in the local church such as that practiced, for instance, by Jonathan Edwards, and revivalism which depended upon the work of itinerant evangelists, such as George Whitefield, who were not accountable to an ecclesiastical body. While we believe the theology of the latter to have been in fundamental accord with the teachings of the Westminster Assembly, his practice of promoting revivals without the assistance or oversight of local churches appears to us to be a clear departure from a high view of the work of the visible church. For that reason, we are inclined to see the First Great Awakening, despite its Calvinistic theology, as being partly out of accord with Presbyterian convictions.

for other denominations. Becoming Baptists, Methodists, and Disciples of Christ, they joined churches where man-centered theology was welcome. Also during the Second Awakening the Cumberland Presbyterian Church was formed, a body whose theology was clearly Arminian.

Controversies over these revivals, coupled with the volatile issue of slavery, led to the split in 1837 between Old School and New School Presbyterians. Old School Presbyterians, largely Scotch-Irish in the middle Atlantic states and the South, were the party of strict subscriptionists. New Schoolers, primarily in New England and the newly settled Midwest were socially activistic, pietistic, and vigorous opponents of all worldliness, from the consumption of alcohol to holding slaves. Later, the outbreak of the Civil War witnessed another split. Old School Presbyterians in the Confederacy split with the Old School Presbyterians in the North and formed their own denomination, reflecting the political divide between North and South. After the defeat of the Confederacy, this body became known as the Presbyterian Church in the US (or, more popularly, as the Southern Presbyterian Church). After the Civil War, Old and New School Presbyterians would reunite, though the Northern and Southern denominations would remain separate until 1983.

The Fundamentalist-Modernist Controversy

The controversies in the Northern Presbyterian Church in which J. Gresham Machen was to play such a crucial role and which would lead to the founding of the OPC in many ways resembled the conflicts of earlier centuries between Old and New Side, and Old and New School Presbyterians. As opposition to the Philadelphia Plan for church union indicates, conservatives like Machen argued for strict subscription to the Westminster Confession, refusing to treat Calvinism as a mere difference of opinion. Yet there was something decidedly different about the fundamentalist controversy. Here the division was not between confessionalists and revivalists, though Presbyterian fundamentalists in the revivalist tradition like Billy Sunday and William Jennings Bryan did not see eye to eye with Machen. Rather, the conflict was be-

tween the naturalism of theological liberalism and the supernatu-
ralism of both confessionalists and revivalists.

After the Civil War, intellectual and social developments undermined confidence in traditional understandings of the gospel.
Darwinism and newer scientific methods of studying the Bible
(i.e., higher criticism) led many to question the uniqueness and
truthfulness of Scripture. Liberal Protestants who welcomed many
of these ideas still believed the Bible was true and special, but did
so more by interpreting the Bible symbolically and by looking to
Christ's ethical teachings as the core of the gospel. Meanwhile, as
American industry mushroomed and attracted immigrants from
around the world to work in the nation's rapidly expanding and
congested cities, the gospel's offer of security in the next world
looked increasingly irrelevant to life in this one. An influential
number of Protestant ministers responded to this social crisis with
a social gospel. They attempted to apply Christian ethics to the
difficulties created by industrialization and the urban plight of an
ethnically diverse labor force. They believed Christianity offered
hope for the salvation of society. Jesus may save sinners, they acknowledged, but new social realities required a newer gospel. In
the process, political reform took the place of proclaiming the
good news of salvation in Christ.

J. Gresham Machen, the chief figure in the founding of the
OPC, grew up in a society very much shaped by the optimism and
confidence of America's emerging industrial social order. Born in
1881 to a prominent Baltimore family—his father and older brother were accomplished lawyers—Machen was reared in the Southern Presbyterian Church (PCUS). While this southern
denomination was generally more conservative than its northern
counterpart, the congregation in which the Machen family were
members was thoroughly infused with the progressive spirit of the
time. Machen's distinguished education as an undergraduate at
Johns Hopkins University—an institution which regarded scientific research as part of the nation's march toward righteousness—
did little to question the activistic optimism of American Protestantism. Even at Princeton Seminary, where Machen enrolled after a year of graduate study in the classics at Johns Hopkins, he
failed to see clearly the threat that liberalism posed. He was much
more interested either in attending college football games or in his

studies toward a Master of Arts in philosophy from Princeton University.

Only when Machen went to Europe from 1905 to 1906 to pursue advanced study in New Testament at German universities did he begin to comprehend the threats, both intellectual and social, to Presbyterian orthodoxy. In the fall of 1906 he returned to Princeton Seminary to teach Greek and New Testament. He also began monumental studies of the virgin birth of Christ and the apostle Paul's theology, both of which would be published as rigorous scholarly endeavors. And in the course of his teaching and studies Machen became convinced that liberalism not only denied the fundamental convictions of Presbyterian faith but, more generally, was an entirely different religion from historic Christianity.

Machen summarized this argument in his classic book, *Christianity and Liberalism*, published in 1923. In this work he wrote that Christianity was a religion of grace. Human nature was essentially sinful, leaving men and women in a position where they deserved eternal punishment for breaking God's law, and could do nothing for their salvation apart from the gospel of Christ's atoning death and resurrection. Liberalism, however, said just the reverse. It held that human nature was basically good and that Christ's teaching provided a supreme model for human goodness. While Christianity proclaimed God's marvelous grace in Christ, liberalism appealed to human morality.

The Presbyterian Controversies

The fundamentalist controversy within the Presbyterian Church began in earnest in 1922 when Harry Emerson Fosdick, a liberal Baptist minister preaching regularly at New York's First Presbyterian Church, accused conservatives of intolerance. He said that orthodox views about the virgin birth, the inspiration of Scripture, the atonement, and the second coming of Christ were all matters open to interpretation. And because the interpretation of these doctrines was not fixed, liberals and conservatives should be tolerated in the church.

A little more than a year later, Fosdick's sentiments were echoed in the infamous Auburn Affirmation written in December of 1923. Claiming to protect the "unity and liberty" of the Presbyterian Church, this declaration was signed by over 1,200 ministers and denied the right of the church to establish certain fundamental truths as tests of theological orthodoxy. According to the Affirmation, views such as the infallibility of the Bible, the virgin birth of Christ, his substitutionary atonement and bodily resurrection, and miracles were not facts essential to the Bible but merely theories about Scripture's message. Conservatives like Machen countered that such skeptical views about truth denied not just the confessional character of the church but even the authority of Scripture.

To end the growing antagonism within the church, Charles Erdman, professor of practical theology at Princeton Seminary and moderator of the 1925 General Assembly, appointed a commission to study the causes of division within the church and make recommendations to restore "purity, peace, unity and progress." After a year of investigation, the committee reported back to the general assembly that no traces of liberalism could be found in the denomination and that the cause of controversy was due to conservatives who made unfounded accusations against well-intentioned and sincere Presbyterian ministers. The committee completely ignored Machen's testimony which pointed to the 1920 plan for church union, Fosdick's preaching, the Auburn Affirmation, the ordination of two New York ministers who denied the virgin birth, and the lack of conservatives on denominational boards and agencies as evidence that liberalism was present in the church.

Though the Special Commission's report did not single Machen out by name, it did state that conservatives were responsible for dividing the church. The General Assembly of 1926 focused on Machen, however, when it appointed a committee to investigate dissension at Princeton Seminary. As the fundamentalist controversy unfolded, the faculty and administration divided into two camps: the moderates, led by Charles Erdman and J. Ross Stevenson, and the conservatives, headed by Machen, William Park Armstrong, and Caspar Wistar Hodge (all members of the faculty), and Clarence Macartney (a member of the seminary's board of directors). The moderates were by no means liberal. Rather, they were influenced by the revivalist impulses of American evangelicalism and believed that effective outreach and church unity were more important than theological precision or uniformity. From their perspective, there may have been a few liberals in the church—people who did not dot every "i" and cross every "t" of the confession—but standing against them was not worth destroying the unity of the denomination. Conservatives, however, saw liberalism as a message antagonistic to the gospel. How could any church that took the Bible and theology seriously willfully tolerate error in its ranks?

Other issues were also at stake in the debates at Princeton. The seminary had been an agency of the Old School Presbyterian Church. When the Old and New Schools reunited in 1869, the plan allowed Princeton to retain its Old School theological identity. Old School Presbyterianism stood for strict adherence to the Westminster Confession and an insistence that, according to Presbyterian polity, the church, not parachurch agencies, was the only acceptable means for conducting the work of missions and evangelism. Moderates at Princeton in the 1920s, however, came from New School backgrounds, and wanted the seminary to represent the whole church, not just Old School Presbyterianism. For Machen and other conservatives, the issue was not just the legal matter of following the seminary's constitution; it also involved the meaning of Christianity itself. Was the Westminster Confession of Faith the system of truth revealed in the Bible, as the ordination vows of the Presbyterian Church stated? If it was, then preserving the Old School character of Princeton concerned not just technical legal matters but the meaning of the gospel. Princeton, in conservative minds, stood for the truth of the gospel as revealed in Scripture. Others who wanted the seminary to change did not see the value of Presbyterian orthodoxy.

In 1929 the contest for the identity of Princeton Seminary— and more generally for the identity of the Presbyterian Church— came to an end. The seminary was reorganized in such a way that conservatives who had been a majority on the board of directors were now a minority. What is more, signers of the Auburn Affirmation were appointed to serve on Princeton's board. In effect, the seminary had been forced to conform to the theologically tolerant—if not indifferent—character of the Presbyterian Church. Princeton Seminary, an institution that had stoutly served the Reformed faith since 1812, Machen wrote, had been lost to the cause of Presbyterian orthodoxy.

In response to these devastating developments, Machen and other conservatives in the Philadelphia vicinity founded Westminster Theological Seminary. Yet, according to Machen, speaking at the seminary's opening exercises in the fall of 1929, "Princeton Seminary is not dead, the noble tradition of Princeton Seminary is alive." The new seminary would endeavor "by God's grace" to continue the Princeton tradition unimpaired, as he explained,

> . . . not on the foundation of equivocation and compromise, but on an honest foundation of devotion to God's Word, to maintain the same principles that old Princeton maintained. . . . that the Christian religion, as set forth in the Confession of Faith of the Presbyterian Church, is true; and . . . that the Christian religion should be proclaimed without fear or favor, and in clear opposition to whatever opposes it, whether within or without the church, as the only way of salvation for lost mankind.

Such was the founding vision for Westminster Seminary. This was also the founding vision for the OPC. For Machen founded a new seminary not just to add diversity to the world of higher education but in order to train Presbyterian ministers who, week in and week out, would proclaim the whole counsel of God as set forth in the Westminster Confession of Faith. In a few years it would be painfully clear that the ministers trained at Westminster would not be welcome in the Presbyterian Church and that a new denomination would be necessary. That denomination would be the OPC, a church dedicated to faithfully following Scripture, adhering to Old School Presbyterianism in its worship, polity, and doctrine, and putting faithfulness to Christ above the success of numbers or the plaudits of the world. This vision for the OPC was shaped by the developments within Presbyterianism of the 1920s, events which taught that constant vigilance is necessary for the vitality of the church, that errors must be continually expelled, that purity of doctrine, worship, and life must be the goal. In sum, this vision was to be a Presbyterian church, nothing less.

2
The Founding of the Orthodox Presbyterian Church

AFTER THE EVENTS of the 1920s and the loss of Princeton Seminary to concessive forces within the Presbyterian Church, Machen became convinced that conservatives would have to start thinking about a new church. As early as 1924 he believed verbal adherence to the Bible and the confession of faith would not assure orthodoxy. But once the very boards and agencies of the church began to combat the gospel in their official activities, then the need for a new church would be clear.

In 1932 the scenario which Machen feared became a reality. This was the year *Re-Thinking Missions* was published, a massive evaluation of world missions funded by John D. Rockefeller, Jr., and co-sponsored by the missions boards of seven Protestant denominations, including the Presbyterian Church. The report recommended that the churches reconceive their mission strategy. The authors denied the exclusive nature of the Christian faith and favored an approach that acknowledged good in all religions. Missionaries, they said, should not work for the "destruction of [other] religions" but for "their continued co-existence with Christianity, each stimulating the other to their ultimate goal, unity in the completest religious truth." Christianity was not a religion distinct or hostile to other world religions. Rather, it was the fulfillment or the perfection of universal religious sentiments. The report also argued for a new conception of the missionary enterprise. Evangelism should no longer be the motive for missions. Instead, humanitarian services such as education and medicine had religious value in and of themselves. To shower other lands with these blessings was to Christianize them as much as to call individuals to faith and repentance.

In his history of this period, *The Presbyterian Conflict*, Edwin H. Rian writes that *Re-Thinking Missions* was premised on the modernist assumption "that the germ of truth exists in all religions and that it is the duty of the missionary to recognize that germ of truth as the least common denominator and build thereupon." The church had outgrown the work of missions. No longer were missionaries to show the false character of other religions and to point people to the one way of salvation. It seemed offensive to the modern, enlightened mind to preach the unique claims of Christ and to assert that other religions were simply false. For modernists the traditional missionary activity was cultural imperialism, and the religious traditions of native peoples must be respected, not challenged.

The controversy that erupted after the publication of *Re-Thinking Missions* had all the earmarks of the 1920s fundamentalist controversy. Conservatives in the church believed that the Presbyterian Church's Board of Foreign Missions, which had two of its members on the committee that wrote the report and which refused to condemn its conclusions, was guilty of harboring liberalism. Moderates who were concerned to keep the church unified and programs afloat opposed conservative accusations as distractions from the positive work of the church. Liberals never really had to get involved in the fight since conservatives and moderates were disagreeing so well on their own. The result was a dispute between faithfulness to Scripture and the confession, and the effective outreach of the church—theological integrity versus pragmatic efficiency.

But the missions controversy of the 1930s took on a different tone from the debates of the 1920s when Machen and several other conservatives founded in 1933 the Independent Board for Presbyterian Foreign Missions. At this point the battle for Presbyterian orthodoxy shifted to a contest over Presbyterian polity. Just as the events of the 1920s, in which leaders like Machen defended Calvinist theology, were important for shaping the OPC's confessional identity, so the skirmishes of the 1930s over Presbyterian church order were crucial for the OPC's characteristic dogged adherence to Presbyterian practices in ecclesiastical politics.

Presbyterian Polity

There are dozens of denominations in existence today that claim to be Christian, yet all of them adhere to one of three kinds of church polity. There are hierarchical churches, such as Roman Catholic and Episcopalian. These denominations order the offices of the church in a hierarchy: bishops, priests, and deacons. Furthermore, they claim that authority in the church is found in direct and uninterrupted apostolic succession. Another common form of government is the congregational model, found, for example, in Baptist churches. This teaching affirms the autonomy of the local church. Each congregation is independent, responsible only to Christ as its head, and is not subject to church councils.

The third model for church government is Presbyterianism. Presbyterians believe that the Bible requires the church to be governed by elders. More recently some Presbyterians have argued that the Bible describes only two offices for the maintenance of the church, namely elders and deacons; e.g. Lawrence R. Eyres, *The Elders of the Church* (Phillipsburg: Presbyterian and Reformed, 1975). But historically, Presbyterianism has taught that Jesus Christ by his Spirit instituted the office of the minister of the Word, or teaching elder, along with the ruling elder and the deacon for the preservation of sound teaching and good order in his church. This is commonly called the "three-office" view. The minister is called in Scripture "preacher," "pastor," "teacher," "steward of the mysteries of God," and in this combination of functions is distinct from the elder. The minister does rule, along with the elders, but unlike the elders he does not earn his living in secular occupations but is supported by the church because his life is devoted to preaching the Word (I Cor 9:14, "those who preach the gospel should receive their living from the gospel").

In Presbyterian polity, the local church is governed by a session that is composed of the pastor and ruling elders. The church is also a member of a regional group, a presbytery, uniting the pastors and ruling elders of a region. Finally, there is the general assembly, which is the governing body of the whole church, composed of such ministers and ruling elders as the presbyteries shall commission to it. These bodies—the session, presbytery, and general assembly—all exercise discipline and oversight over the church. The system of lower and higher judicatories preserves the peace and unity of the church while protecting the rights of the local assemblies.

Unlike the congregationalists, Presbyterians seek the visible unity among congregations. In contrast to hierarchical churches, the unity is structured through representative and non-hierarchical means. Presbyterians believe that Christ alone sovereignly rules the church, as the Westminster Confession states, "There is no other head of the church but the Lord Jesus Christ." The confession adds that church government is designed for the edification of the church and that believers are to receive the church's decisions "with reverence and submission" if "consonant to the Word of God."

The Independent Board
for Presbyterian Foreign Missions

Questions about Presbyterian polity and the authority of the church lay at the heart of the missions controversy of the 1930s. Convinced that the Presbyterian Church's Board of Foreign Missions tolerated and in some cases promoted liberalism, Machen in 1933 through his regional body, the Presbytery of New Brunswick (NJ), overtured the general assembly to instruct the missions board to do all in its power to insure that sound missionaries and doctrine were characteristic of its activities. To make his case clearer, he also wrote a lengthy pamphlet, "Modernism and the Board of Foreign Missions of the PCUSA." In it he argued that *Re-Thinking Missions* was "from beginning to end an attack upon the historic Christian faith." Beyond the Foreign Missions Board's own endorsement of the report, Machen also pointed out other ways the board was condoning modernism.

Perhaps the most glaring example of modernism within Presbyterian foreign missions was Pearl Buck. The well-known author of *The Good Earth* and other novels, Buck lived in China and taught in Nanking University under the aegis of the Board of Foreign Missions. As a thoroughly committed modernist, she urged the church to rid itself of "the old reasons for foreign missions." These reasons were adherence to doctrines such as original sin, the deity of Christ, his substitutionary atonement, and his resurrection, all of which she linked to "superstition" and "magic religion." Machen insisted that the integrity of the board required it to dismiss her and other modernists from the rolls of Presbyterian missionaries. He made it plain that this was not an esoteric issue before the church, stating that "the real question is what the Board of Foreign Missions is doing with the funds which the Bible-believing Christians, at great sacrifice, are entrusting to it."

While foreign missions became the battleground, it would be a mistake to think that this was the only area of the church affected by modernism. On the contrary, it was the perception of the conservatives that the church's Board of Foreign Missions was the *least* contaminated of the official boards. According to the *Presbyterian Guardian*, the literature produced by the Board of Christian Education contained "unvarnished paganism," and the Board of National Missions had the highest percentage of Auburn Affirmationists of all three boards.

Machen's overture was defeated by the Presbytery of New Brunswick, but a similar measure came before the 1933 General Assembly from the Presbytery of Philadelphia. It too was defeated through what conservatives believed was an outright evasion of the issue for the purpose of protecting the church's image. The clear message was that unbelief was institutionalized in the church. One of Machen's students at the time, Robert Churchill, described the moment as one in which the church had effectively rewritten Galatians 1:8 to read, "If any man preach another gospel, let him be supported."

Rebuffed by the ordinary means of Presbyterian procedure and convinced that other more visible means of combatting modernism were required, on June 27, 1933, only four weeks after the general assembly, Machen and his supporters organized the Independent Board for Presbyterian Foreign Missions for the expressed purpose of promoting "truly Biblical and Presbyterian mission work."

Was the formation of the Independent Board a wise decision? This question is not easily answered. Machen's high view of the church and the accountability normally insured by Presbyterian polity made the establishment of what was essentially a parachurch organization for the work of missions an anomaly at best. Even though the officers of the board were all Presbyterian and the

missionaries they supported had been ordained Presbyterian ministers, the board was not directly answerable, as Old School Presbyterians would have insisted, to the visible church in anything
more than an informal way. But while uncomfortable with the
board's independence, Machen believed the dire situation in the
church required an emergency measure. According to Robert
Churchill, the Independent Board was never intended to be permanent. It would be dissolved if and when the official board reformed. The Independent Board was a temporary effort to address
the desperate state of missions in the church. Moreover, the centralization and bureaucratization of many of the Presbyterian
Church's ministries, missions being only one example, severely re-
stricted efforts to reform denominational agencies by removing
them from the more immediate supervision of church courts.

A more troubling concern for Machen and the supporters of
the board was the division the board provoked within the conservative cause. Many conservatives within the church, especially
some members of Westminster Seminary's faculty and administration, equally opposed to modernism, argued that the Independent
Board was too antagonistic and that it did not serve the best interests of the cause of orthodoxy. Sadly, some of these allies deserted
the cause over disagreement on strategy. The irony was that these
supporters had gone along with the founding of Westminster, an
independent Presbyterian institution. From Machen's perspective,
organizing the Independent Board was no different from establishing Westminster Seminary. Emergency situations required unusual
tactics. And the only way to make the church take notice was to
establish institutions committed to the Reformed faith and unfet-
tered by the denomination's desire for acceptance within American culture.

The Word of God versus the Word of Man

Ultimately, the debate over the Independent Board shifted to
the ecclesiastical question. Here the independence of the board
was critical. Machen believed that the central agencies and offices
of the denomination had become too powerful and too much subject to the whims of a small modernist party within the church.
The centralization of the church's bureaucracy had made it in-

creasingly difficult for conservatives not just to shape denominational policy but even to have a voice in denominational affairs. More and more denominational officials were subverting church polity and procedure in order to force their own agenda upon the church at large. According to Machen,

> Everywhere we find centralization of power under an arbitrary bureaucracy; the idea of liberty is slowly but very surely being reduced. Solemn contracts . . . are being treated as scraps of paper; the solid foundations of liberty and honesty are crumbling beneath our feet. . . . The Church, bearing the sacred name of Christ, is standing on a lower ethical plane than that which prevails in the world outside—than that which prevails among people who make no profession of religion at all.

These problems had been evident in the Special Commission of 1925's rulings and the reorganization of Princeton Seminary, but assumed a particular urgency in the case of the fundamentalist Presbyterian, Donald Grey Barnhouse, pastor of Tenth Presbyterian Church, only a few blocks from Westminster's original center-city Philadelphia campus. In 1930 he had begun a series of Sunday evening services in an area theater that drew people away from their own services and caused ministers in the vicinity to object. Especially offensive was Barnhouse's declaration that he would sooner die than allow a liberal minister to preach in his pulpit. Liberals within the Presbytery of Philadelphia eventually brought Barnhouse to trial for breach of the ninth commandment and violation of his ordination vows. He was found guilty and was admonished by his predominantly conservative presbytery, the lightest punishment under Presbyterian law.

Machen was by no means a supporter of Barnhouse, a minister partial to dispensational premillennialism and indifferent to Westminster—but Machen was alarmed by the proceedings, believing it would set an important precedent. From his perspective, the church court had ruled that the minister's utterances were slanderous without ever considering whether they might be accurate. The trial was a clear signal to church members that disloyalty to the Presbyterian Church or its ministers would result in charges being brought against dissenters. Machen wrote in one letter that the ruling was "an outrage" and added that if Barnhouse were guilty, all conservatives were guilty. The trial raised the possibility that conservatives would be forced to make common cause with modernists.

The issues of constitutionality and restraint of arbitrary power came up forcefully in the aftermath of the organization of the Independent Board. Could the church prohibit the action of its members to form agencies independent of the church? On this issue Machen's conservative critics agreed; whether or not the formation of the Independent Board was prudent, Machen was acting fully in accordance with the constitution of the Presbyterian Church to organize the new missions board. What is more, the church had never questioned the support that local congregations sent to independent missions agencies such as the China Inland Mission.

Yet church officials, some of whom had signed the Auburn Affirmation, took a different view of the Independent Board. The stated clerk of the general assembly, Lewis Mudge, opined that the new agency subverted Presbyterian law by undertaking "administrative functions within the church without official authorization." He also instructed presbyteries that graduates of Westminster Seminary could not be licensed to preach unless they affirmed the commitment to support the official work of the denomination. Machen pointed out that such demands for loyalty to church agencies was clearly unconstitutional—ordination vows could not be amended without the consent of the church through its ordinary deliberations. In addition, demanding such a pledge of loyalty was tyrannical—it obligated ministers to support whatever denominational agencies did. Above all, it was unbiblical—it substituted the word of man for the Word of God.

Having eliminated the potential of support for the Independent Board, Presbyterian officials next acted against the board itself. In the spring of 1934, the members of the Independent Board were instructed that the new organization was in violation of the church's constitution and that board members were guilty of violating their "ordination or membership vows, or both." The basis for this decision came in *Studies of the Constitution of the Presbyterian Church in the U.S.A.*, a document prepared for the 1934 General Assembly. This booklet placed the broadest possible construction upon the power of the general assembly. It also stated that offerings to the denomination were as much an obligation as the celebration of the Lord's Supper. Gifts could only be given to organizations approved by the general assembly. This interpretation of Presbyterian polity was ratified by the 1934 General Assembly, which also ordered the members of the Independent Board to resign their positions. If they did not comply, they would be brought to trial.

Conservatives, whether members of the board or not, were outraged. Maitland Alexander, a former director of Princeton Seminary, said, "if we are to have a Presbyterian Mussolini, give us one with Mussolini's brains. . . . if we are to have a Pope, give us one with the wisdom and conservatism of the Vatican." Samuel G. Craig, a member of Westminster Seminary's board, wondered whether the general assembly had ever read the Westminster Confession which declared that " 'decrees and determinations' of synods and councils 'are to be received . . . if consonant to the Word of God.' " The general assembly's action, according to Clarence Macartney, was an "invasion of Presbyterian liberty" and "another victory for modernism."

The Presbytery of New Brunswick asked Machen to comply with the edict. He refused and responded with a prepared statement. Machen objected that the church's mandate made church benevolences a tax and that the general assembly had illegally granted itself the power to interpret the constitution and confession without the ratification of lower courts. Presbyterian law safeguarded the rights of individuals and lower judicatories from "the tyranny of the higher." This law was also premised upon the notion of due process. But the entire question of the Independent Board's constitutionality had been decided without giving the board's members a day in court to hear their side. The decision therefore violated basic Protestant principles, clearly substituting human authority for the Word of God and, in effect, adopting the Roman Catholic Church's view that the seat of authority in religion is "the Bible interpreted authoritatively by the church." In effect, the ruling instructed ministers to take their Bibles from their pulpits and use instead the last Minutes of the general assembly. Machen concluded that the Independent Board had not violated Presbyterian law, and the unconstitutional methods of the church hierarchy proved as much.

Despite his vigorous defense, Machen and the rest of the Independent Board were eventually brought to trial. In Machen's case the proceedings began in February 1935. His counsel tried to hold up the trial on a variety of legal matters in order to show how unethical the whole affair was—for instance, no conservatives were on the judicial commission which heard the case and the commission had wanted to conduct the trial in private. There was even a question whether the Presbytery of New Brunswick was the proper court of jurisdiction. Machen had transferred to the Presbytery of Philadelphia in 1934, but the stated clerk of the general assembly, also a member of the Presbytery of New Brunswick, ruled that Machen's transfer had been invalid because the proper paper work had not been filed. In all likelihood, the conservative Presbytery of Philadelphia would not have brought Machen to trial, or at least would have made such a proceeding very messy for the denomination.

If Machen and his counsel thought some of these matters indicated a lack of fairness, they had no idea what was ahead. After settling these technicalities, Machen's counsel, H. McAllister Griffiths, prepared to take up the heart of the matter, namely, whether the official Board of Foreign Missions was condoning modernism and, if so, could someone be convicted of lying and violating his ordination vows for pointing this out. But before he could say a word, the commission ruled that it would hear no evidence concerning modernism in the church, the soundness of the Board of Foreign Missions, the Princeton-Westminster controversy, or the legality of the 1934 mandate. With Machen unable to defend his actions, the commission, on March 29, 1935, found him guilty as charged and recommended that he be suspended from the ministry unless he repent of his indiscretions.

Machen responded that the commission had simply condemned him without a hearing. He had disobeyed the 1934 mandate, a "purely arbitrary administrative order," because it was unconstitutional. The only way to test a ruling, he added, was through the courts, beginning with the presbytery. The Presbytery of New Brunswick, however, had refused the right of such testing. The entire case came down to this, he said: "I am ordered by the General Assembly to support the modernist propaganda which is being furthered by the official Board of Foreign Missions. . . . Being a Christian man, I cannot do so."

In the aftermath of this trial and ones similar to it, approximately one hundred ministers and elders gathered at Philadelphia in June 1935 to form the Presbyterian Constitutional Covenant Union. The organization was designed to combat the growing influence of those who supported the Auburn Affirmation and to protest the outcome of the Independent Board member trials. Covenant Union members vowed to make every effort to reform the denomination. If these endeavors failed, they would "perpetuate the true Presbyterian Church . . . regardless of cost."

The PCCU was committed to the notion that doctrinal and administrative matters could not be separated. Presbyterian leaders could not be content with preaching the gospel to their congregations or insuring that local churches remained sound; they had to take their grievances to church councils because Presbyterian polity insisted upon the theological uniformity and integrity of the church. The church was not a pluralistic institution. Its message was bound by the Westminster Confession of Faith. And making one's concerns known at presbytery and general assembly was the way to insure such unity. The one prime requisite for anyone taking part in this movement, Machen told one timid supporter, "is that he shall be a fighter." The cause of true Presbyterianism would die of inaction unless conservatives kept up the "ecclesiastical fight."

For Machen and the PCCU, this fight ended in June 1936 when the general assembly upheld every verdict against the members of the Independent Board. It ruled that the Independent Board "expressly contravened provisions of the constitution and did great harm to the peace of the church." Machen's "denunciations of fellow-ministers" amounted to defamation of character and "seriously aggravated his other offenses." The commission directed the Presbytery of New Brunswick to suspend Machen from the ministry.

Only ten days following the close of the general assembly, the PCCU convened in Philadelphia and the new denomination was formed. The OPC was constituted with thirty-four ministers and seventeen elders. Machen was elected its moderator and immediately affirmed the principles for which he and other conservatives

had been fighting since the 1920s. The new church would maintain and defend the Bible "as the Word of God," the Westminster
Confession of Faith "as the system of doctrine taught in Holy
Scriptures," and the principles of Presbyterian church government
"as being founded upon and agreeable to the Word of God." With
the formation of the new church came a sense of relief. "What a
joyous moment it was," Machen sighed, "how the long years of
struggle seemed to sink into nothingness compared with the peace
and joy that filled our hearts. We became members, at last, of a
true Presbyterian Church."

Machen had good reason to experience relief. The founding of
the OPC was the culmination of years of hard fought controversy
and the product of considerable time, energy, and money. Many
had questioned Machen's character and had hurled a variety of in-
sults at the conservative movement. Yet what made the founding
of the OPC so welcome was that it fulfilled Machen's view of the
responsibility of the church. Machen expressed that view in 1932
before the Academy of Political and Social Science:

> The responsibility of the church in the new age is the same as its re-
> sponsibility in every age. It is to testify that this world is lost in sin;
> that the span of human life—nay, all the length of human history—
> is an infinitesimal island in the awful depths of eternity; that there
> is a mysterious, holy, living God, Creator of all, Upholder of all, in-
> finitely beyond all; that He has revealed Himself to us in His Word
> and offered us communion with Himself through Jesus Christ the
> Lord; that there is no other salvation, for individuals or for nations,
> save this, but that this salvation is full and free, and that whosoever
> possesses it has for himself and for all others to whom he may be the
> instrument of bringing it a treasure compared with which all the
> kingdoms of the earth—nay, all the wonders of the starry heavens—
> are as the dust of the street.
>
> An unpopular message it is—an impractical message, we are told.
> But it is the message of the Christian Church. Neglect it, and you
> will have destruction; heed it, and you will have life.

Machen and the OPC

One cannot understand the OPC's emphasis on doctrine
without an appreciation of the doctrinal crisis out of which the
OPC arose. For Machen and his supporters, irreconcilable differ-

ences in belief lay at the heart of the controversy. The theological views of modernists and Christian orthodoxy were mutually exclusive. For the sake of the purity of the church, separation was necessary. And the struggles in which Machen engaged go far in explaining the character of the church. The OPC, since its founding, has been characterized—by friend and foe—as "the little church with the big mouth." Certainly, Machen's desire for a doctrinally sound church is no formula for explosive church growth in a pragmatic and anti-intellectual age that is hostile to sound theology. Moreover, the church must be wary of proudly boasting of its small size as a sign of its unswerving fidelity to the truth.

Yet the OPC *has* survived, and more than that, it has maintained its commitment to the Westminster Confession and Presbyterian polity. Like its founders it has heeded the admonition of Paul: "Watch your life and doctrine closely. Persevere in them, because if you do, you will save both yourself and your hearers" (I Tim 4:16). This is unmistakably a sign of God's grace, and for that the church must be truly thankful.

3
The Division of 1937

WHEN THE OPC WAS FORMED on June 11, 1936, hopes ran high among a small number of Presbyterians who, for the better part of a decade, had struggled against modernist unbelief and had followed J. Gresham Machen out of the mainline Presbyterian Church. In his editorial for the *Presbyterian Guardian*, Machen tapped this optimism when he wrote, "With what lively hope does our gaze turn now to the future! At last true evangelism can go forward without the shackle of compromising associations." Yet, for all his enthusiasm, Machen was also cautious. As a good Calvinist, he knew well that the new church would not be immune to the sins which stalk the human heart. So in his sermon before the OPC's First General Assembly in 1936, he warned that while the OPC was a "real part of the Church of God" it was nonetheless a "little company of weak and sinful folk."

Machen's words before the commissioners who gathered in Philadelphia for the First General Assembly were as prophetic as they were descriptive. Behind the scenes, the OPC was engaged in an intense struggle that would be crucial for the denomination's mission and future.

At first glance, controversy within the new church would seem the least likely development. After all, these Presbyterians had been accused of fomenting controversy and division within the mainline church. To demonstrate that they were interested more in faithfulness than in power, the leaders of the OPC wanted their new church to reflect the fellowship and common purpose that the gospel of Christ commands and produces. Also, having a common enemy and experiencing a sense of liberation from the dead hand of modernist theology and from the underhanded tactics of denominational officials should have paid off with large dividends of trust, commitment, and unity.

But among the many lessons that church history teaches is that when new churches are founded, the result often is not unity but greater fragmentation. For instance, despite opposition to the abuses and false teaching of the Catholic Church, the Protestant Reformation produced such different expressions of Christianity as Lutheranism, Anabaptism, Anglicanism, and Presbyterianism. So too, opposition to Protestant modernism in the Northern Presbyterian Church yielded diverse forms of conservative Protestantism. As events in the months before and after the OPC's founding would reveal, the conservatives who joined the new denomination had different reasons for opposing modernism and, as a result, different understandings of what the new church should be. During the first year of the OPC's existence, conflicts over the church's identity became readily discernible. These conflicts not only involved Machen's own vision for the new church but, more importantly, went to the heart of what it meant to be faithful to God's Word as taught by the Westminster Standards.

Conservative Fragmentation

Put simply, the controversy that fractured the OPC during its first year concerned a choice between American fundamentalism and the Reformed faith. If one defines fundamentalism strictly by its opposition to modernist theology, then the OPC is and always has been a fundamentalist denomination. But by such a definition conservative Lutherans, Episcopalians, Anabaptists, and even Roman Catholics would also qualify as fundamentalist, for conservative communions in those theological traditions have also opposed efforts to adapt the church's teaching and practice to modern secular culture.

Fundamentalism, however, has a more precise definition than the mere opposition of liberalism. It also stands for certain theological emphases, among which are dispensationalist theology, revivalistic techniques of soul-winning, stern prohibitions against worldly entertainments, and a low view of the institutional church. The most important feature of fundamentalism that played havoc in the division of 1937 was dispensational premillennialism.

Dispensationalism is a way of interpreting the Bible that divides redemptive history into various ages (dispensations). In each period, according to this view, God establishes a covenant with his people, his people in turn break the terms of that covenant, and God punishes such sinful behavior with a catastrophic form of divine judgment. Dispensationalism also features a fair amount of interest in the end of the current and last age—the time between the apostles and the end of human history—known as the age of the church. Consequently, dispensationalists spend much time trying to understand what biblical prophecy teaches about the end of this age. According to dispensationalism, the age of the church will be just like other dispensations. God's people will fail to keep the covenant and divine judgment will end the age of the church. But unlike other dispensations, Christ will return and establish his kingdom, thus inaugurating the millennium, his thousand-year reign. This is why dispensationalists are premillennialists. They believe that Christ will return before the millennium (as opposed to postmillennialism, i.e., Christ's return will come at the end of the millennium).*

Dispensationalism's chief architect was John Nelson Darby, an Anglican minister in the Church of Ireland, who eventually established the Plymouth Brethren. Owing to his tours in the United States and Canada during the late nineteenth century, dispensationalism became fairly popular among Northern Presbyterians and Baptists. The publication of the Scofield Reference Bible in 1909 by Oxford University Press also contributed greatly to the spread of dispensational views among Protestants who opposed liberalism. For many of these believers, dispensationalism seemed to make perfect sense of the social decay that they saw in America.

---

* Not all premillennialists are dispensationalists. Historic premillennialists are different from dispensationalists. Historic premillennialism, like dispensationalism, teaches that Christ will return to establish a one thousand-year reign on earth. But unlike dispensationalism, historic premillennialism does not break the history of redemption into various stages. Consequently, it does not involve the idea that God has dealt in a variety of ways with his people at different periods of history.

Urbanization, industrialization, and immigration had transformed the United States from a fairly stable and homogeneous nation into one beset by poverty, crime, and distrust. History was not improving, contrary to what many postmillennialists and liberal Protestants believed. Rather, signs everywhere indicated that sinful men and women were disregarding God's law. The only hope for improvement lay in Christ's return when he would judge disbelief and iniquity. The task of believers was to save as many unbelievers as possible before the day of judgment.

Dispensational theology thus performed a valuable witness to historic Christianity. At a time when naturalism became the norm for modernist theology, dispensationalism preserved the supernatural character of the gospel. When many Protestant scholars were beginning to view the Bible as an inspirational book written by culturally conditioned human authors, dispensationalism nurtured a high view of Scripture as God's word of salvation to sinners. Furthermore, at a time when many mainline Protestants saw the American nation as the visible manifestation of God's kingdom, dispensationalism sometimes encouraged a healthy skepticism of the so-called progressive ways of the United States.

But as important as dispensationalism was for building opposition to liberalism, it also harbored a number of teachings that were at odds with the Reformed faith. Especially troublesome was the idea that God dealt differently with humankind during different historical periods. Reformed theology teaches that ever since the fall, salvation comes only through Christ, the Messiah promised to Israel and revealed in the New Testament to the church. But dispensationalism implies that God uses different means of salvation at different times, thus denying the finality of the fall and the continuity of redemption throughout the Bible. During the 1920s and early 1930s when conservative Presbyterians and dispensationalists had a common enemy, these differences were not apparent. But by the time of the OPC's founding in 1936, points of controversy had begun to surface in ways that turned out to be explosive and divisive.

Machen himself had been critical of dispensationalism in his popular book *Christianity and Liberalism*. There he called it "a false method of interpretation of the Word of God" and argued that the prophecies of the Bible could not be "mapped-out" in as definite a fashion as dispensationalists taught. Nevertheless, Machen went on in the same book to point out "how great" his agreement with dispensationalists was in regard to the authority of Scripture, the deity of Christ, and the supernatural character of grace. "Christian fellowship," he concluded, "with loyalty not only to the Bible but to the great creeds of the Church" could still unite Presbyterians and dispensationalists. The dangers of modernism were so great, however, that Reformed believers and dispensationalists during the 1920s rarely studied what divided them.

During the 1930s as conservative Presbyterians began to establish their own institutions, such as Westminster Seminary and the Independent Board for Presbyterian Foreign Missions, rather than merely attacking liberalism, more consideration had to be given to the beliefs for which conservatives stood. And as conservatives struggled to erect the boundaries of the movement, Machen began to see more clearly the serious ways in which dispensationalism undermined the Reformed faith and, in fact, that theological differences separated fundamentalists and Presbyterians which could not be harmonized. At the same time, the leaders of the OPC fully embraced the teaching of amillennialism as the view on Christ's return most consistent with Scripture. Unlike premillennialists, who looked to Christ's second coming as the beginning of his thousand-year reign, and postmillennialists, who believed Christ would return at the end of a thousand-year period of prosperity for the church, amillennialists, as John Murray explained, held that Christ's second coming would mark the end of this age and the beginning of "the eternal age, when the kingdom of God will have been consummated." That age would not be a literal millennium nor would it be the reign of God on earth. Instead, Christ's second coming, or the "day of the Lord," would be eternal and would bring the dissolution of the present heavens and earth, thus inaugurating the new heavens and new earth prophesied in II Peter 3:14.

The Controversy

In the fall of 1936 through a series of relatively benign coincidences, these differences came to the surface. The controversy intensified when R. B. Kuiper, a professor of practical theology at

Westminster Seminary, reported on the OPC's First General Assembly to the Christian Reformed Church to which he still belonged. It would have warmed the hearts of Dutch Calvinist ministers, he wrote, to hear OP ministerial candidates questioned about "the two errors" which were "so extremely prevalent among American fundamentalists," namely, Arminianism and the Dispensationalism of the Scofield Reference Bible. Carl McIntire, an OP pastor in southern New Jersey, in his church paper, the *Christian Beacon*, took exception to Kuiper's published remarks. He claimed that the majority of the OPC was premillennialist and that the church was committed to "eschatological liberty." He added the warning that a "premillenarian uprising" would ensue if Kuiper did not cease his "veiled and continued attacks."

Machen thought McIntire's editorial was politically unwise; he was especially critical of the New Jersey pastor's unwillingness to publish a response by Kuiper, something demanded by "journalistic ethics as well as by the ethics of the Bible." Nevertheless, the more important issue was not political but theological. Machen feared that McIntire was turning premillennialism into an "*essential* doctrine." And in a letter to another premillennialist, J. Oliver Buswell, an OP minister and president of Wheaton College, Machen took aim at the Scofield Reference Bible—a book he regarded as "profoundly harmful." The "root error" of dispensationalism, Machen wrote, was its "utter failure" to recognize "that anything irrevocable took place when Adam fell." He admitted that he had not always felt so strongly, having devoted most of his life "to the refutation of naturalistic Modernism." The Scofield teaching had always seemed "a side issue," but not so "erroneous as to be opposed to Christianity." With the formation of the OPC, however, he saw that many of the laity treated Scofield's notes as though they were God's Word; he also believed that dispensationalism was dominating preaching. Machen hoped that the OPC would turn "from these elaborate schemes" to the "grand simplicity" of the Reformed faith.

Disputes about dispensationalism revealed two distinct camps within the leadership of the OPC—one side Old School Presbyterian in outlook, the other fundamentalist. The Old School party, led by Machen, consisted of the majority of Westminster's faculty, many of whom came from non-American Reformed traditions

such as Scottish Presbyterianism (John Murray), and Dutch Cal-
vinism (Cornelius Van Til, Ned B. Stonehouse, and R. B. Kuiper).
This group was characterized by a high regard for the Westminster
Confession, Presbyterian polity, and Reformed piety (e.g., liberty
in various matters such as beverage alcohol and tobacco, where
Scripture is silent). The fundamentalist party was led by Carl
McIntire, J. Oliver Buswell, and Allan MacRae, professor of Old
Testament at Westminster. Though Buswell and MacRae dis-
avowed the dispensationalist label, this group was premillennialist
and defended the liberty of OP congregations to use the Scofield
Reference Bible. They also were less rigorous in their application
of Presbyterian polity and promoted a form of piety that featured
abstinence from liquor, tobacco, movies, dancing, and cards.

At its Second General Assembly, held in November 1936,
these parties managed to avoid a breach, even though McIntire
threatened to split the church. Machen tried to keep the two sides
together, despite his own Old School sympathies, and orchestrated
the election of J. Oliver Buswell as moderator. Still, theological
controversy could not be avoided. As the church took up the matter of its constitution, two issues emerged which reflected the
growing division within the OPC.

The first matter concerned which version of the Westminster
Confession the OPC would adopt. In 1903 the mainline Presbyterian Church had amended the confession with two new chapters—one on the Holy Spirit and the other on the love of God and
missions. The OPC general assembly decided that these amendments were Arminian in character and should be eliminated from
the version of the Confession it would adopt. This was the prevail-
ing view of Machen and his Old School colleagues at Westminster
Seminary. But this decision drew some opposition from fundamentalists, many of whom were involved in court battles over church
property. By revising the confession, they argued, it would be hard-
er to convince public authorities that the OPC was the genuine
successor to the Presbyterian Church and that its congregations
should keep their property. Many of those who voted to eliminate
the 1903 revisions were also engaged in property disputes, but for
them theological integrity mattered more in the long run than re-
taining church buildings.

The second issue concerned eschatology. A number of overtures and reports expressed the desire for "eschatological liberty"
within the OPC, that is, sufficient room for different views of
Christ's return and the millennium. But the Old School party, as
well as the moderator, Buswell, thought that the Westminster
Standards should stand on their own without any extra provisions.
And since the Westminster Confession only teaches that Christ
will come again, the church was already committed to allowing
different views of the millennium as long as those views did not
conflict with the Reformed theology taught by the confession.
Thus, even though the general assembly appeared to grant the liberty that some dispensationalists desired, it actually kept the controversy over premillennialism alive. For many in the church
believed that dispensational theology was at odds with the Westminster Standards, not with regard to the millennium, but more
importantly over the effects of the fall and the unity of God's gracious ways throughout redemptive history.

While the Second General Assembly did not give the Old
School party a clear victory, it did make the church's Calvinistic
confessional identity explicit. The body eliminated the 1903
amendments to the Westminster Confession which were at cross
purposes with the Reformed theology of the standards. The general assembly also refused to cave in to dispensationalist pressure and
go beyond the Westminster Standards on questions surrounding
the time and nature of Christ's second coming. Suffering from this
setback, the fundamentalist party retaliated by taking control of
the Independent Board for Presbyterian Foreign Missions. Even
though the independence of the board from ecclesiastical oversight suggested that the conservative missions agency condoned
non-Presbyterian forms of church government, the board's constitution stated that it would support only those missionaries who
vowed to conduct and establish missions based on the Westminster Confession and "the fundamental principles of Presbyterian
Church government." The board's independence at its founding
in 1933, then, was merely a temporary measure to protest the desperate state of the mainline denomination's missions enterprise. In
other words, despite its independence, the board was committed to
establishing and conducting Presbyterian, *not* independent, missions.

The fundamentalist takeover of the Independent Board, however, appeared to compromise the agency's commitment to Presbyterian church polity. At its annual election of officers in the fall of 1936, fundamentalists on the board, especially McIntire, fearing that a Westminster clique had taken control of the OPC, successfully ousted Machen as the board's president, a position he had held since its founding. They elected instead Harold S. Laird, pastor of an independent church in Wilmington, Delaware, and named another independent minister as vice-president. McIntire's group was now in control of the board. Machen was deeply distressed. Close associates and family members believed that he was so hurt by the action of the board, an organization upon which he had risked his reputation, that his physical strength was seriously depleted, making him an easy prey for his fatal illness. Still, in his last letter to Buswell, Machen did not reveal his sorrow. Instead, he wrote that the Independent Board was at "the parting of the ways between a mere fundamentalism, on the one hand, and Presbyterianism on the other." The board's elections had revealed that it was now in the hands of dispensationalists. This led to the withdrawal of OP support for the Independent Board the following year.

The last issue that split the OPC concerned Christian teaching on personal morality. Specifically, the church was divided over total abstinence from alcoholic beverages. While this issue might seem foreign to Christians living at the end of the twentieth century, most American Protestants had supported vigorously the Eighteenth Amendment to the United States Constitution, an act which prohibited the production and sale of beverage alcohol and which was not reversed until 1933. So whether Christians could drink in good conscience was still a hotly contested matter when the OPC was founded.

Debates about total abstinence came to a head at the 1937 General Assembly, though the issue had been lurking in the background for some time. Fundamentalists such as Buswell and McIntire were displeased by the Westminster Seminary faculty's unwillingness to condemn liquor. The faculty held that to advocate total abstinence was to reject the example of Christ, who at the wedding of Cana (John 2) changed the water into wine. Nevertheless, rumors circulated throughout the church that seminary students drank in their rooms with the approval of the faculty. It did not help matters that several of Westminster's faculty also smoked tobacco. While debates about the consumption of alcohol and tobacco concerned the significant matter of the Bible's teaching on Christian liberty, the breach within the OPC also reflected cultural differences. A majority of Westminster's faculty came from non-American backgrounds where drinking and smoking in moderation were acceptable. What is more, Machen had been a vigorous opponent of prohibition and was known to bring cigars to faculty meetings even though he did not smoke them himself.

Nevertheless, despite these cultural differences, an important aspect of Christian practice was at stake. At the Third General Assembly, Buswell threatened withdrawal if the denomination did not renounce drinking. Two overtures came before the assembly— one urging total abstinence came from Buswell's Presbytery of Chicago; the second argued that simple adherence to the Westminster Standards was as far as the church could go. Each side appealed to Scripture, to precedents in American Presbyterianism, and to Machen's own practice and convictions. In the end, Buswell's overture lost by a large margin. The OPC based this decision on the principle that Christians should be free to follow the dictates of their own consciences in "matters where the Bible has not pronounced judgment." Immediately following the assembly in May 1937, fourteen ministers and three elders, led by Buswell and McIntire, withdrew from the OPC and in 1938 formed the Bible Presbyterian Synod.

Assessment

The division of 1937, despite its roots in the aftermath of the fundamentalist controversy, parallels remarkably a split that shook American Presbyterianism a century earlier. In 1837 the Presbyterian Church also split into two rival communions, the Old School and New School Presbyterian Churches. The issues of the compatibility of the Westminster Confession with evangelical theology, the importance of Presbyterian polity, and divergent understandings of Christian liberty contributed to the 1837 split just as they did in the OPC's division of 1937. And both cases revealed the tensions between the Reformed faith and American evangelical-

ism. Just as the Old School party in the OPC rejected dispensationalism for contradicting the Reformed understanding of the fall
and the covenant of grace, so the Old School Presbyterian Church
opposed the Arminian theology of Charles Finney's revivals as antithetical to Calvinist theology. Just as the Old Schoolers in the
OPC made Presbyterian polity an issue when they withdrew support from the Independent Board for Presbyterian Foreign Missions, so the Old School Presbyterian denomination insisted that
the visible church, not parachurch organizations, should oversee
and regulate evangelism and missions, and therefore refused to cooperate with the voluntary associations of the Second Great
Awakening. And just as Old Schoolers in the OPC opposed fundamentalist efforts to prohibit on religious grounds the consumption of alcoholic beverages, so their forebears in the nineteenth
century also criticized the moralism and legalism of extreme aboli-
tionists and prohibitionists.

In both the Old School-New School split of 1837 and the
1937 division of the OPC, then, we can see significant differences
between Reformed convictions and American Christianity in the
revivalist tradition. Where Reformed churches stress human depravity and the sovereignty of God in salvation, evangelicals have
overestimated human initiative and underestimated the pernicious effects of sin. Where Reformed churches insist that the
means of grace be supervised and regulated by church officers,
evangelicals have resisted such restrictions as too confining and
ineffective for reaching the widest sphere of influence. And where
Reformed churches have been unwilling to go beyond Scripture in
condemning specific practices, evangelicals in their condemna-
tion of certain activities have often been influenced more by the
surrounding culture than by Scripture. Just as these tensions pre-
cipitated a split between Presbyterians in the early part of the
nineteenth century, so they also revealed the differences between
members of the OPC committed to the Reformed faith and those
informed by the theology and practices of American fundamentalism.

Some thought that Machen's premature death on January 1,
1937, contributed to the division of the OPC. His sudden death
from pneumonia while traveling to Bismarck, North Dakota, to
rally support for the OPC robbed the new church of its most capa-

ble leader. As Ned Stonehouse wrote in the January 23, 1937 issue of the *Presbyterian Guardian*, probably the most moving piece written on Machen's death, the deceased "was far more than a brother to many of us. He was a father in Israel and we have become orphans." Indeed, Machen's leadership in the formation of Westminster Seminary, the Independent Board for Presbyterian Foreign Missions, and the OPC made him "chief among equals." Stonehouse went on to observe that Machen "was notably the spiritual father of a generation of theological students who crowded his classrooms," and he had profoundly affected their "thinking and living." The void created by Machen's death was great. "We have depended so much upon him in the past," Stonehouse lamented, "that it might well appear that we could not go on without him." But even though his "steadying hand" was gone, Machen's "devotion to truth and duty" left a heritage of "complete devotion to principle" which would help the church to "go on under God in loyalty to the truth for which [Machen] gave his life."

Had Machen lived, perhaps he could have provided the stability and leadership necessary to find a compromise. His own activities in the church controversies of the 1930s, however, reveal that compromise would have been difficult. Even before his death, significant disagreements emerged between him and both Buswell and McIntire. Machen had a history of resisting compromise with all his might and main when the basic positions of the Reformed faith were being attacked. Also, the takeover of the Independent Board by McIntire demonstrated important differences that could not easily be resolved. From its inception the OPC was faced with a choice between being Reformed and being fundamentalist. From Machen's perspective there was never any doubt about what the church should be. He had left Princeton to found Westminster in order to perpetuate the training of Old School Presbyterian ministers. And he helped to found the OPC as a church in which Westminster's graduates could minister. As it turned out, the Reformed identity of the OPC after the division of 1937 was virtually identical to Machen's original vision for the church.

The name of the denomination, in fact, spoke volumes about this vision. When the denomination was first founded, its name was the Presbyterian Church of America. Machen had argued that this title reflected the church's claim to be the spiritual successor to the mainline denomination. But in 1937 the Presbyterian Church in the USA took the new denomination to court, charging that people might confuse the two denominations because of similar names. In 1938 the court ruled in the PCUSA's favor, and the leaders of the new denomination were forced to look for another name. Various ones came before the Fifth General Assembly: The Evangelical Presbyterian Church, The Presbyterian and Reformed Church of America, The North American Presbyterian Church, The Presbyterian Church of Christ, The Protestant Presbyterian Church of America, and The Free Presbyterian Church of America. In 1939 the commissioners chose "The Orthodox Presbyterian Church." The decision was fitting for it reflected the church's theological and ecclesiastical commitments.

In fact, Machen himself as early as 1935 chose the term "orthodox" as the proper adjective for describing the movement in which he played such a vital part. "Fundamentalism," he wrote, was inadequate because it failed to do justice to the great heritage of Augustine, Calvin, and the Westminster Confession. "Conservative" was unsatisfactory because it gave the impression of "holding desperately to something that is old merely because it is old." "Evangelical" was not sufficiently clear; it did not designate those who held specifically to the Westminster Standards. But "Orthodox" was fitting because the word "orthodoxy" meant "straight doxy," or correct thinking. To see whether a doctrine was "straight" it had to be compared against the "plumb line" of the Bible. As Machen argued and as the division of 1937 revealed, the rule for the OPC's "straight doxy" was the Word of God. The OPC defended and adhered to the Reformed faith not because it was old or because it had such great champions as Augustine or Calvin; rather, it was committed to the Westminster Confession because, as Machen declared, it is "the creed which God has taught us in his Word."

In the end, Stonehouse's words of consolation at the time of Machen's death turned out to be prophetic. The division of 1937 revealed the OPC's true colors and the heritage of "complete fidelity to principle" which Machen had left to the church. The OPC had been founded not merely because the mainline church tolerated liberalism but because Christ instituted the church to proclaim the whole counsel of God. And for the OPC, proclaiming the whole counsel of God involved the system of doctrine and polity taught by the Westminster Standards. The church was established not on the basis of fundamentalism but out of a deep commitment to and love for Calvinist theology, Presbyterian church government, and Reformed piety.

PART TWO
MISSIONS

AS the previous section showed, missions was at the heart of the OPC's founding. The early leaders of the denomination were not only concerned to send out missionaries who would proclaim a Christian message; they also wanted missionaries who would not be afraid to preach the whole counsel of God. And for the early generation of Orthodox Presbyterians, the whole counsel of God meant Presbyterian theology and polity, not a broad evangelical-ism.

Some may have wondered about Machen's intentions during the controversy over missions. After all, he could have been using the storm over the "Layman's Inquiry" and Pearl Buck merely to prove his point about the corruption of the Presbyterian hierar-chy, while not being all that interested in the cause of foreign mis-sions per se.

But Machen's interest in missions, and particularly in the way that liberalism was undermining the effort to take the good news of the gospel to non-Christian lands, was evident well before the 1930s when he helped to found the Independent Board for Pres-byterian Foreign Missions. In *Christianity and Liberalism* (1923) Machen wrote,

> The missionary of liberalism seeks to spread the blessings of Chris-tian civilization (whatever that may be), and is not particularly in-terested in leading individuals to relinquish their pagan beliefs. The Christian missionary, on the other hand, regards satisfaction with a mere influence of Christian civilization as a hindrance rather than a help; his chief business, he believes, is the saving of souls, and souls are saved not by the mere ethical principles of Jesus but by His re-demptive work. The Christian missionary, in other words, and the Christian worker at home as well as abroad, unlike the apostle of lib-eralism, says to all men everywhere: "Human goodness will avail nothing for lost souls; ye must be born again."

The contrast Machen drew between liberal and Christian mis-sions, between emissaries of Western culture and stewards of the gospel, is one that has characterized the OPC's mission effort both at home and overseas. For whatever reason, whether in reaction to the missionary endeavors of liberal Protestantism or because of zeal for faithfulness to Scripture, the OPC has always been wary of substituting American cultural norms and values for the proclamation of the Word. As the following chapters make clear, the OPC has not always practiced what it preached. But in the main the denomination has been mindful of the differences between the work to which Christ called the church, that is, the ministry of word and sacrament, and the functions which God ordained other institutions to perform.

Thus, the stories in this section of the OPC's labors in establishing churches in the United States, the Far East, and Eritrea testify to the church's commitment to obey Christ's command to take the gospel to the lost. Of course, we tell only a fraction of the full story of OP missions. The OPC has been Christ's witness in Philadelphia, in America, and to the ends of the earth. Space prevents us from mentioning many home and foreign missionaries, and many places, such as Portland, Oregon, and Abilene, Texas, or the Middle East, Suriname, and the Philippines. Though necessarily selective, these chapters capture how the OPC's Reformed convictions apply to the challenge of missions and render the church's efforts distinctive. Unlike liberal Protestants who abandoned the proclamation of the gospel for the establishment of culture, and unlike evangelicals and fundamentalists whose zeal for the gospel was sometimes betrayed by a weak view of the visible church, the OPC maintained a high commitment to reaching the lost with the good news of Christ through the God-ordained means of establishing churches characterized by the preaching of the Word, the administration of the sacraments, and the exercise of discipline.

4

Home Missions

AT THE FOUNDING of the Orthodox Presbyterian Church, only three congregations who engaged in battles with the PCUSA over property rights won the right to retain their property. The prospect of losing their property kept many churches, otherwise sympathetic toward Machen, from joining his cause. Those that did left beautiful and historic buildings to worship in unusual surroundings. Orthodox Presbyterians in Middletown, Pennsylvania, met in the Post Office. The Hamill, South Dakota, church met in the hayloft of a barn. In Leesburg, Virginia, it was the Police and Fire Department building, and in Gresham, Wisconsin, a former saloon. Others found space in hotels, American Legion Halls, movie theaters, private homes, or rented storefronts. Far removed from the popular image of Presbyterian churches, where the stately edifice of "First Presbyterian" sits prominently in the town square, these humble beginnings confirmed in the new denomination a sense of cultural disenfranchisement.

During this time the Presbyterian Church in the USA had launched an ambitious program in home missions. Its Board of National Missions employed a full-time church architect and poured millions of dollars annually into new churches. In contrast to this, the OPC embarked on a concerted effort to establish new churches despite extremely modest financial resources. Among the first acts of the inaugural general assembly of the Orthodox Presbyterian Church was the creation of its Committee on Home Missions and Church Extension (CHMCE). The diligent work of the committee in those trying circumstances prompted Robert Marsden, in his early history of the OPC, *The First Ten Years*, to label it the "backbone of the Orthodox Presbyterian Church."

The Franklin Square Story

New York was among the most liberal presbyteries in the PCUSA at the time of Machen's departure, and so it was not surprising that none of its congregations left it for the OPC. Yet establishing a congregation in the New York metropolitan area was a priority for the new church's Committee on Home Missions and Church Extension.

The denomination was less than a year old when evangelistic meetings began in New York City in January of 1937. Area surveys indicated that the most strategic location would be in the Long Island community of Franklin Square, in the middle of Nassau County, three miles east of the city border. The first service was held on January 29, 1939, in the American Legion Hall, with twenty-one people in attendance. Among the worshipers were Robert and Elizabeth Wallace, recent immigrants from Northern Ireland. Ten months later the church was received into the Orthodox Presbyterian Church as a particular congregation, with twenty members and two ruling elders, including elder Wallace.

Largely relying at first on Westminster Seminary faculty and students for pulpit supply, the church called Bruce Coie as its first pastor in 1942. In 1943, through the assistance of the denomination's Home Missions Committee, property was purchased on Franklin Avenue, a main artery that connected the northern and southern shores of Long Island, one block south of the Hempstead Turnpike, a major east-west route. The property included a brick and concrete building with full-length basement, as well as four additional lots. Soon afterwards the church purchased a manse.

Long Island would change rapidly after World War II as automobile travel prompted massive urban exodus. Franklin Square was suddenly transformed from a farming community into a densely populated suburb. In 1945 Robert Vining was called; his gifts matched well the growth of the area in the baby boom era. Gradually, the church would gain greater financial stability. In 1948, it completed payments on its five-year building loan from the Home Missions Committee. By 1950 it had become entirely self-supporting.

Elmer Dortzbach, noted for his rapport with young people, was called as pastor in 1952. The church continued to grow in attendance, requiring larger worship space. In 1955 a new building was completed on the north end of the property, connected to the existing facility. The red brick sanctuary with laminated wooden arches in the interior was both simple and attractive. When the balcony was completed it provided seating for 250 persons. Six years later the church added a nursery wing.

In 1957 it called its fourth pastor, and John C. Hills began his twenty-two year tenure as pastor of the Franklin Square church. With his extraordinary preaching gifts, Hills led the church into a deep maturing of its love for the Reformed faith. In 1971 a number of families living in Westchester County, north of New York City, expressed a desire for a Reformed work. In response, Hills began a series of weekly Bible studies in New Rochelle. Eventually, that effort would become a particular congregation of the OPC in 1983. Franklin Square has also sought to extend its witness to eastern Long Island. In 1984 worship services were started in a chapel in Lindenhurst in Suffolk County. Although services were suspended after a couple of years, the church still hopes to start a work in Suffolk County in the near future.

After Hills's death, Franklin Square called William Shishko in 1981. Under his leadership an annual fall Bible conference was begun. A parent-controlled Covenant Christian School was formed in 1984 and began to meet on the church property.

From its founding, the Franklin Square church has experienced a pattern of slow, steady growth. From twenty members at its founding, it grew to about one hundred by 1955, and in recent years it has maintained steady levels around 150. Its reputation for solid biblical preaching, a strong teaching program, and commitment to the nurturing of the covenant youth is well established in the denomination. Included among its covenant youth are two great-grandsons of Robert and Elizabeth Wallace.

"Preserving the Results of Local Evangelism"

In 1942 the general assembly formed a committee to instruct the church on the methods of establishing new churches. The result was a series of wide-ranging studies on local evangelism, which included reports on survey work, group evangelism, circuit missions work, radio preaching, and other topics. One of the most illuminating aspects of the committee's work was its report entitled "Preserving the Results of Evangelism," which was its description of a successful church extension work.

In order for the fruits of evangelism to be preserved, the report suggested, individuals and families must be nurtured and edified in the faith. Full instruction in the faith should take the form of four to eight membership classes that precede a credible profession before the church's session. The last membership class did not end the work of evangelism, however. Instead, the report argued, the evangelistic task needed to be followed with a systematic program of Christian nurture. New Christians must establish habits to encourage godly living, including Christian fellowship and reading sound Christian literature. The Christian faith must be firmly established in the home, and the whole family must be under the ministry of the church. "Essential supplements" of an evangelism program included congregation visitation, a Christian school, faithful exercise of church discipline, and the establishment of a church lending library.

Particularly noteworthy were two features of the Christian life "which the average young Christian is in serious danger of neglecting." These were the keeping of the Christian Sabbath and the daily discipline of Bible reading and prayer. The report was unambiguous and forthright in its sabbatarian convictions: "The proper keeping of the Lord's Day by the young convert is probably the most important single element in truly preserving the results of evangelism."

Finally, the report urged that the new believer be inoculated from the threat of secularism by establishing a Christian world and life view: "A robust Christian theism is our heritage. We are to set forth the God who is sovereign in all dimensions of life. There is no possible area of life that is neutral. All of life owes its true meaning to God the Creator and Sustainer."

In this report, the OPC defined an Old School approach to evangelism in contrast to an evangelical one that reduced evangelism to decisions for Christ. It understood evangelism to be a complex process with elements that merged with Christian nurture. The purpose of evangelism was not merely conversion, but the development of Reformed and Presbyterian sensibilities in new believers. Without these steps, the church could not expect to survive as a genuine expression of Presbyterian piety, and the work of evangelism would prove unfruitful. The very language of the report was revealing. Rather than employing the (now familiar) term "church growth," the report spoke of the "establishment" of churches, a phrase suggesting more spiritual depth than numerical growth.

As young churches such as Franklin Square would implement these programs, a certain ethos would develop in the OPC. Congregational piety took on a self-consciously Reformed shape in the early history of the church, as members participated in Machen Leagues for young people, Women's Missionary Societies, Vacation Bible Schools, mid-week prayer meetings, catechetical instruction, and presbytery-sponsored summer Bible camps.

The New Life Story

If the OPC had established a model of Presbyterian piety in its home missions efforts, did it come at the expense of fuller and more aggressive outreach? Did it have an "ingrown mentality" that targeted white, middle-class suburbia and failed to communicate, for example, with the disillusioned younger generation that was alienated from the established church? These questions prompted a group, under the leadership of C. John Miller, to form New Life Presbyterian Church in Jenkintown, Pennsylvania, in 1973.

New Life had some similarities with Franklin Square. Both featured strong preaching ministries, led in each case by a minister with a reputation for public eloquence. Both churches had a strong commitment toward missions, with heavy financial support for both home and foreign missionaries. But these aside, two more different churches are difficult to imagine.

New Life adopted a nontraditional approach to worship and ministry intentionally targeting the disenfranchised. Worshipers clad in blue jeans would gather in a rented gymnasium to sing to guitar accompaniment praise choruses from overhead projections. Stressing the need to establish strong interpersonal relationships, the church enrolled its members in small group ministries, called mini-churches, that met during week nights. New Life immediately attracted large numbers. Within a year it had 100 members; ten years later, the numbers swelled to nearly 500. By 1987, it had grown to over 650 and had planted two daughter churches. Quickly it had become one of the largest congregations in the denomination.

Another important distinctive of New Life was its pragmatic understanding of Presbyterian polity. In 1987 New Life of Jenkintown and its daughter churches (in northeast Philadelphia and suburban Fort Washington) formed a "New Life Network" in order to create "vital fellowship beyond our local church boundaries." The network was to feature joint worship services, pulpit exchanges, staff coordination, and mutual prayer and financial support. Curiously, all of these were normally the functions of a presbytery. Many in the Presbytery of Philadelphia, already disappointed at New Life's lukewarm support for presbytery efforts, saw the "New Life Network" as divisive—in effect, a "presbytery within a presbytery."

Not long after the formation of the New Life Network, the member churches withdrew from the OPC and "voluntarily realigned" with the Presbyterian Church in America, believing that the PCA's more aggressive church planting programs were more conducive to the "outgoing" philosophy of New Life. In a letter to the congregation, the session of New Life of Northeast Philadelphia posed the question, "where does our church 'fit' most strategically, in light of our ministry, our location, and the times in which we live?" The session's answer was that "our affiliation with the PCA is clearly the better option for us." Such options were possible because of New Life's independent mindset that falsely contrasted Presbyterian polity with higher commitments, as evidenced in their claim, "Our loyalty is not ultimately to any denomination, however good it is: neither the OPC nor the PCA. Our loyalty is to Christ and his kingdom."

A comparison between the New Life and Franklin Square congregational experiences is instructive because it demonstrates the dilemma that confronts the Orthodox Presbyterian Church. How can new churches express a dynamic evangelistic thrust without losing their denominational identity? For New Life, the former came at the expense of the latter. For Franklin Square, theological and denominational commitments guided the church to the path of slow growth.

CHMCE: Marketing the Church?

Rather than remaining an isolated case in the church, the innovations of New Life grew increasingly influential in the OPC. An implicit endorsement took place with the appointment of Lewis Ruff to serve as the general secretary of CHMCE in 1982. *New Horizons* described Ruff as "reformed in his theological commitment," yet "willing to examine nontraditional approaches to see if they were helpful in reaching unbelievers." In short order Ruff's nontraditional methods would both gain popularity and produce strife within the church.

Beginning in 1984, Ruff and CHMCE published "Seedtime" as a four-page quarterly insert to the *New Horizons* in order to promote and encourage evangelism in OP congregations. A survey of its contents indicates CHMCE's ambivalence about the Reformed distinctives in evangelism. In addition, "Seedtime" was full of suggestions for maximizing the comfort of church visitors. It reminded members of the congregation to smile at them and it urged ushers to make good first impressions. Bulletin covers should be "exciting," and the facility should appear attractive. "How many have you lost," the editor inquired, "because of appearance?" All of these methods begged the question of whether the unchurched ought to feel comfortable in the presence of a company of believers worshiping an Almighty God.

"Seedtime" advice stressed new techniques. The successful church will exhibit flexibility and spontaneity and "embrace faith in a new future." One contributor urged that Sunday schools should be redesigned as outreach tools, dismissing those Sunday schools that "generally serve only our covenant youth." Other outreach activities included soccer evangelism and church-sponsored recovery programs.

Another strategy for church growth was the introduction of two different worship services—one traditional, the other contemporary. "One of the major barriers to growth in middle-sized churches is their unwillingness . . . to include two different Sunday morning worship experiences. . . . Rather than having to choose another church because of such preference, people can now choose another service."

Furthermore, "Seedtime" advised, the church should work toward avoiding jargon, especially in its advertising: "Most 'outsiders' won't understand terms like glorify, covenant, or triune God, or even fellowship. Why risk misinterpretations of your message?" One way to entice outsiders, it suggested, was to change the congregation's name. "Orthodox" was removed and substituted in its place were the comfortable phrases associated with upscale subdivisions. "Seedtime" also instructed churches to spell out their distinctiveness in the form of "philosophy of ministry" statements. In the examples it cited, congregational distinctiveness was characterized by worship style and the "personality" of the ministry. Entirely lacking was any reference to the denominational or confessional heritage of the church.

In all of these suggestions, the implication was clear: congregational growth was predicated on maximizing its appeal to the unchurched. Whereas former church plants were self-conscious in belonging to a denomination, new efforts were deliberate in muting an OPC identity. CHMCE's ideas proved popular among many in the OPC. A pre-assembly workshop with the church growth consultant Frank Tillapaugh in 1985 was well attended, while a preaching workshop a few years later was canceled due to insufficient registration.

Yet there also emerged growing criticisms of CHMCE's new emphases. The tensions between CHMCE and the church peaked in 1987, when a CHMCE-sponsored advertisement ran in an issue of *Eternity* Magazine with the bold headlines, "She Wants it All!" and featuring an attractive young woman on an exercise machine. The ad copy, which solicited contributions for a program called "Mission America," boasted that the committee was employing "street smart workout techniques" to plant new churches.

Objections to the advertisement prompted a five-hour debate at the general assembly on the strategies and tactics of CHMCE.

Some challenged the prudence of soliciting money from outside the denomination for "visionary evangelistic efforts." Much of the debate was deflected towards the allegedly provocative nature of the ad. Another offense, which regretfully few of the commissioners dwelt on, was the commercialization of the church. By establishing the analogy between church membership and the trappings of American consumerism, CHMCE was selling the church like a commodity.

However one interpreted the advertisement, and the work of CHMCE under Ruff in general, it was clear that, fifty years after the founding of the church, CHMCE was far from the "backbone" of the denomination. For some, it became an embarrassment to the church; for everyone, it was the source of confusion over denominational identity.

Church Growth Reevaluated

Ruff's controversial tenure would end in 1987 when he resigned to accept a call to plant a church in the PCA. In response to a general assembly directive, CHMCE produced an extensive report to the 1988 Assembly that outlined the "Principles, Policies, Methods, and Vision for Church Growth" of the committee. The report identified some strengths and weaknesses of the church growth movement. Among the former, it appreciated the challenge to see the church grow and the understanding of diverse ways in which growth is experienced. Weaknesses included a "numbers-only orientation" and the application of the "homogeneous unit principle" that encouraged churches to segregate according to social, economic, and cultural differences.

The report expressed commitment to biblical church growth principles, stating, "We must choose the evangelistic methods and goals that best glorify God." It defined evangelism in a way that distinguished the roles of both the general office of believer and the special office of minister. Finally, it encouraged the church to engage in methods of a "presbyterian orientation."

In evaluating the report, the assembly's Advisory Committee had some important critiques. It felt that CHMCE failed to identify Reformed distinctives fully. The Advisory Committee said, "We want to see self-consciously Reformed and Presbyterian congregations growing under our church planting efforts." Specifically, it rejected the report's qualified endorsement of "assessment centers," which employed psychological testing to evaluate a candidate's gifts in church planting. According to the Advisory Committee, CHMCE's report confused winsomeness with spirituality, as when it described "personableness, dynamism and friendliness" as "important gifts" in a church planter. The assembly agreed with the judgment of the Advisory Committee, and it instructed CHMCE to "cease to utilize assessment centers."

In 1990 CHMCE appointed Ross Graham as its new general secretary. Soon after he assumed the post, he published in the *New Horizons* a series of ten propositions on "The Bible and Church Planting." Together, the propositions provided a reassessment of church growth and outlined a Reformed approach to church planting. "Too much of the [church growth] literature," Graham wrote, "deals with the church as if it were merely another social organization whose purpose is to grow, develop a myriad of programs, and grow some more. Our Reformed heritage tells us that very often people and size are not the issues."

New churches should be planted with a "fully Presbyterian structure." Both CHMCE and the presbyteries should provide supervision of and support for young churches. Graham was clear that the goal of church planting was a Presbyterian and Reformed product—covenant communities that focused on God-centered worship. While less specific than the earlier study, "Preserving the Results of Local Evangelism," Graham's propositions were a helpful clarification of Reformed principles to a church confused over church planting goals and strategies. Rather than seeking to be "culturally relevant," Graham urged, "let's patiently teach the beautiful doctrines of the Reformed faith."

Conclusion

In summary, the history of the OPC's home mission philosophy reveals a turn toward and a subsequent withdrawal from the pragmatism of American evangelicalism. How fully the church has returned to a self-consciously Reformed and Presbyterian orientation still remains to be seen.

The tension between market-oriented evangelism and Reformed evangelism is one that OP congregations will continue to experience. Much of OP piety is out of step with both American culture and American evangelicalism. Consider, for example, how many evangelical churches sponsor "evangelistically-oriented" leisure activities on Sundays (such as Super Bowl parties) in the interest of convenience. OP churches can mimic these techniques only by jettisoning a sabbatarian consciousness that a previous generation regarded as essential for evangelism.

As New Life experienced, this tension may pit a young church's desire for "outward" community identity against its "inward" denominational identity. The "outwardly-minded" church plant would do well to reflect carefully on the consequences of its approach. Do psychological enticements and sociological techniques replace prayer and providence? Is the message so seeker-sensitive that it gives no offense? Do churches advertise peace and joy by downplaying sin and judgment?

The OPC is not without some success stories, from a numerical point of view. Some churches, like Cedar Grove in Wisconsin, seemed to be engaged in constant building and expansion programs. The Silver Spring, Maryland, church planted a daughter church in Burtonsville in 1969, which went on to plant a granddaughter church in Columbia in 1979. As a whole, however, the OPC has not grown as a denomination into the size that its founders had hoped and prayed. From its founding size of about four thousand members, it has only gradually grown to its present number of nearly twenty thousand.

Growth of the OPC, 1939–1989

Year	Presbyteries	Churches	Members	Ministers
1939	7	64	5,549	64
1949	7	71	7,604	98
1959	8	90	10,233	133
1969	10	116	14,038	170
1979	11	136	15,806	248
1989	12	169	19,422	335

If these numbers are discouraging, the church planting statistics may be even more so. From the founding of the church in 1936
through 1989, over forty percent of the congregations have either
closed or have withdrawn from the denomination. Some plants are
like "shooting stars": they burn brightly for a short time, then burn
out. Some are victims of our social mobility, as key families face job
relocations. Others find that disputes develop before mature elder-
ship can be established. Still others find themselves constricted in
a Reformed denomination. Whatever the reason, America has
proven to be rocky soil for the OPC.

It has been suggested that these statistics should prompt the
denomination to engage in "corporate repentance" over its failures
in evangelism. Perhaps instead, the church should qualify the assumption in the 1988 CHMCE report that the OPC should *expect*
quantitative growth. Perhaps a confessional church should *not* focus on numerical growth in a narcissistic and therapeutic culture.
Can the church sacrifice confessional fidelity for the sake of size?

In the end, the OPC must not lose focus on the true nature of
church growth. In a 1957 article in the *Presbyterian Guardian*, Harvie Conn put it well: "How does a church grow? It grows by its conformity to God's truth, and that is not measured by numbers, but
by the yardstick of growth in grace. . . . Growth is measured by
standards, other than numerical ones. Growth is in grace and in
the knowledge of our Lord and Savior Jesus Christ."

5

Missions to the Orient

WHEN J. GRESHAM MACHEN and other conservatives founded in 1933 the Independent Board for Presbyterian Foreign Missions, the controversy about theological liberalism within the Presbyterian Church in the USA shifted from doctrine to polity. What was the status of the new board? Denominational leaders questioned the constitutionality of an independent missions agency and brought charges of disloyalty against Machen and other board members. From the other side came claims that church leaders who prosecuted Independent Board members were maneuvering the procedures in such a way as to violate not just the rules of Presbyterian polity but also all common-sense notions of fairness. Lost in these questions of legality and procedure were the theological issues which Machen had brought to the fore in his famous book, *Christianity and Liberalism*. Was liberalism, which according to Machen was "an entirely different religion" from Christianity, being taught on the missions field? And if so, wasn't such teaching leading precious souls astray? Again, it was not merely a case of who was right. The theological controversy ultimately concerned how sinners are made right with the holy and righteous God of the universe.

Evidence of the perils that liberalism presented were especially apparent during the 1930s. What had been true of some American Protestant missionary efforts for decades was now being brazenly displayed and defended. Reaching lost souls with the good news of Christ's gracious death and resurrection was no longer a sufficient motive for missions. Increasingly, mainline Protestants were making Western advances in medicine, education, politics, and business the task of missions under the guise of ministering to the "whole man." Ironically, theological liberals ended up becoming as captive to the culture of liberal democracy at the same time they claimed that the authors of the Bible, whose message they discounted, were bound by the norms and assumptions of ancient, pre-modern cultures. And by embracing the patterns of Western society, liberal missionary efforts also proved to be no better on the score of cultural imperialism. While they accused conservatives, who preached absolute devotion to Christ, of being intolerant and insensitive to the claims of native religions, liberals, who were keen on equality, freedom, and democracy, rarely appreciated the social arrangements and cultural traditions of non-Western peoples.

As we saw earlier, one indication of liberalism's increasing influence upon foreign missions came in the infamous report, *Re-Thinking Missions* (1932). Here representatives of mainline Protestant missions boards argued that missionaries should be willing to abandon preaching and evangelism in favor of education and other philanthropic initiatives. The message of *Re-Thinking Missions* was soon echoed by Pearl Buck. She applauded the report and criticized older rationales for missions. The traditional emphasis upon conversion, sin, and grace needed to be replaced by medicine, agriculture, education, engineering, and the like. For her, Christianity was essentially the amelioration of human suffering and social injustice. And Christ was not a savior from sin, but the inspiration for the ethical ideals which would bring the triumph of human happiness and social progress.

J. Gresham Machen, well before the missions controversy of the 1930s, articulated a dramatically different idea of the missionary enterprise. In *Christianity and Liberalism* he contrasted the fundamental difference between liberal missionaries and true evangelists—between emissaries of Western culture and Christians who proclaimed the good news of Christ and him crucified. But just when *Re-Thinking Missions* was being debated and Pearl Buck was seconding the report's sentiments, Machen wrote an essay entitled "The Christian View of Missions" which drew the proverbial line in the sand between liberal and Christian missions. One particular paragraph bears repeating:

One thing is perfectly clear—no missionary work that consists merely in presenting to the people in foreign lands a thing that has proved to be mildly valuable in the experience of the missionary himself, which he thinks may perhaps prove helpful in foreign lands in building up a better life upon this earth, can possibly be regarded as real Christian missions. At the very heart of the real Christian missionary message is the conviction that every individual hearer to whom the missionary goes is in deadly peril, and that unless the message is heeded he is without hope in this world and in the dreadful world that is to come.

These, then, were precisely the issues which led to the founding of the OPC. In fact, it is not at all an exaggeration to say that the denomination came into existence because of a profound desire to see the Word of God proclaimed faithfully in foreign lands. It is also not surprising that the OPC's original work in foreign missions would be shaped by the disputes within the Northern Presbyterian Church about liberalism. While the Presbyterian Church in the USA would continue on the path of reducing the gospel to virtues of American society, the OPC would make every effort in its missionary work to keep the proclamation of the gospel central and free from the dictates of culture, whether American or that of the foreign land. This is not to say that OP missionaries upon entering other lands assumed an altogether different identity, one completely separate from American patterns. But the OPC's commitment to the spiritual and other-worldly character of the gospel meant that its missionaries understood their chief loyalty as being to Christ, not to the expectations of Western or non-Western societies.

The story of the OPC's missionary efforts in the Orient makes this point emphatically. Especially in the case of Bruce Hunt, the OPC's first missionary to Korea, we see remarkable evidence of the difficulties which Christ's ambassadors have experienced when forced to choose between loyalty to their Lord and Savior and the government of the host society. And while the stories of OP missions to Japan and Taiwan lack the drama of Hunt's courageous stand for Christ in Korea, these efforts also demonstrate tellingly the church's commitment to put the claims of the gospel above those of culture, no matter what the consequences.

Foreign Missions Committee Established

As we have already seen, the OPC was formed amidst the controversy in Presbyterian foreign missions. It was natural, then, for
foreign missionary work to be a prominent concern for the new
church. Much of the constituency of the church came from the
members of the Independent Board for Presbyterian Foreign Missions, who were disciplined by the PCUSA.

Among the priorities of the new church was the right ordering
of its missions program. The First General Assembly of the OPC
in 1936 appointed a committee on foreign missions. When that
committee reported to the second assembly in the same year, it
recommended that "in view of the existence of the Independent
Board for Presbyterian Foreign Missions . . . nothing be done by
this committee relative to the establishment of an official Board of
Foreign Missions." In commending the Independent Board, the
committee urged congregations to support it. However, as we noted, within a year the leadership of the Independent Board moved
it in non-Presbyterian directions. The committee reported to the
1937 General Assembly that "it does not find itself able any longer
to recommend the Independent Board . . . as an agency for the
propagation of the Gospel as set forth in the Westminster Standards." Accordingly, the OPC established a Standing Committee
on Foreign Missions to oversee its missionary efforts.

The establishment of this committee was significant because
it steered OP missions in a non-parachurch direction, setting the
church apart from other American evangelical missions agencies.
The parachurch character of evangelicalism is perhaps nowhere
more evident than in foreign missions. There are over three hundred independent missions agencies in the United States. Many of
them are doing important work that supports the church, such as
Bible translation and distribution of Bibles and evangelistic literature. Further, many argue that these agencies are more effective
precisely because they are independent of the restraints of church
bureaucracies and politics. But what this logic ignores is the biblical doctrine of the church. God ordained the church as the means
for accomplishing the task of world missions. It was the church
that sent forth missionaries in the New Testament. As Paul wrote,

it is *through the church*, not missions societies, that the manifold wisdom of God should be made known (Eph 3:10).

Sharing these concerns over the changing character of the Independent Board, several missionaries from that agency transferred in 1938 to the OPC's Committee on Foreign Missions. In fact, most of the OPC's original missionaries came from the Independent Board: the Rev. and Mrs. Richard B. Gaffin, the Rev. R. Heber McIlwaine, the Rev. Egbert W. Andrews, the Rev. Malcolm Frehn, and the Rev. and Mrs. Henry W. Coray. All but Frehn transferred from the Independent Board, and all of them served in the Far East: the Gaffins, the Corays, and Andrews went to China, and Frehn and McIlwaine to Japan.

The case of Bruce Hunt and his wife, Katharine, who ministered among Koreans in Manchuria (what is now northeast China), is especially interesting because it illustrates the OPC's decisive break with mainline Presbyterian missions. When the Presbyterian Church in the USA suspended Machen from the ministry in 1936 because of his refusal to leave the Independent Board, it also took action against Hunt, then a 33 year-old, second generation PCUSA missionary to Korea. Like his father, Hunt had studied at Princeton Theological Seminary. There he met Machen and grew both in his commitment to foreign missions and in his love for the Reformed faith.

In 1936, at the time of the OPC's founding, Hunt was on furlough studying at Westminster Seminary, which providentially placed him in the thick of the ecclesiastical struggle. At the April meeting of the Presbytery of New Brunswick, although he himself was under care of the PCUSA Board of Foreign Missions, Hunt protested vigorously the pledge of support to this board which the presbytery required of candidates for the ministry. He agreed with Machen that requiring support of the authorized boards of the PCUSA was an "extra-constitutional question" that the presbytery had no right to ask. The presbytery denied Hunt his right to protest this action and instead charged him with disloyalty.

For Hunt these actions clearly indicated that the PCUSA was no longer faithful to the Word of God, and in fact had put loyalty to denominational agencies above faithfulness to Scripture. He could hardly be called to suffer for the gospel, he reasoned, if he did not represent the true gospel. And so Hunt withdrew from the church and joined the OPC. At the same time, he resigned from the Board of Foreign Missions and came under the care of the Independent Board for Presbyterian Foreign Missions. After the controversies within the Independent Board, which significantly changed the character of that institution, Hunt transferred his membership to the OPC's Committee on Foreign Missions and in 1938 resumed his work in Korea under the new denomination's auspices.

Korean Missions: Trials from Without and Within

Manchuria and the Korean peninsula below it lie within the range of Japanese, Chinese, and Russian power and, thus, vulnerable to invasion. When Japan annexed these areas early in the twentieth century, its Imperial Constitution at first granted freedom of religion to Christians. Yet, in an effort to coerce the Koreans into becoming more faithful subjects, the Japanese undertook a systematic attempt to persecute Korean Christians.

Ironically, this control helped the growth of the church among Koreans in at least one respect. Because of the common antagonism toward the Japanese invaders, Koreans tended not to view American missionaries as cultural imperialists, reserving that charge for the Japanese. Instead, Koreans viewed Americans as fellow sufferers. In the years before World War II, Hunt was busily engaged in itinerating and church planting. During that time, he witnessed both the growth of the church as well as the growing danger to Christians as the world moved toward war.

The strategy by which the Japanese intended the eradication of Christianity in Korea was that of "shrine worship," mandating that all Koreans participate in the worship of the emperor-god of Japan. The government pressured the 1938 General Assembly of the Korean Presbyterian Church to declare its official conformity to the demand that shrine worship be obligatory to all Koreans, including Christians. Under orders of the Japanese police, when the question of shrine worship was put to the floor of the assembly, only the affirmative votes were noted and no negative vote was called. Protests by Hunt and others against this illegal action were ignored, and some who protested were arrested by attending policemen.

The church was thrown into a crisis of persecution and apostasy, but the growing threat did not slow Hunt down. He had established a reputation for possessing an inexhaustible supply of energy, traveling regularly to speak to over twenty groups that totaled over seven hundred people. His remarkable pace in itinerating and planting churches was captured in a letter to the foreign missions committee: "I don't know how much territory I have covered, but it is plenty—walking, cycling, riding on cart, sleigh, truck, bus, and train; yes, even boats."

In correspondence with family and friends, Hunt expressed gratitude for the growth of the church despite the mounting persecution. In 1939 he wrote that the situation was a test for the church and God's means of purifying and strengthening it. "We have been saddened by the threats which have caused fear and the constant falling off of numbers of those meeting in some of our groups, but we are rejoicing to see the strengthening of the faith of those who, having been so tried, have nevertheless continued."

Increasingly, he indicated the growing danger to his own well-being. He was constantly followed by the police, in danger of arrest and imprisonment, occasionally threatened with assassination, and urged by friend and foe to leave the country. He assured his supporters at home "that we are not distressed, that though perplexed, it has not been unto despair, that we have not been forsaken or destroyed, that on the contrary, the work has leaped forward beyond what it had been in any previous year."

Finally, Hunt's fears were realized when he was arrested on October 22, 1941. His prison autobiography, *For a Testimony*, powerfully recollects his sufferings which included the loneliness of solitary confinement, the lack of food and water, and the discomforts of sleeping on a hard floor in sub-zero weather with his cloak as his only blanket. His captors did offer him a way out, if he would recant his testimony. He refused and expected to die in prison. As a 38 year-old father of five children, he longed to return to his family. Naturally, Hunt reflected on the opportunities that he had to return to America as many of his friends had urged. Was it foolish to stay? "During the past two or three years I had been urging them, men, women and children, to be faithful unto death. I had been encouraging them to suffer anything rather than bow to shrines where the emperor was worshiped as a god." He had wit-

nessed firsthand the beatings and imprisonments of his fellow
Christians. "Could we take our family out of it and leave the Koreans to suffer alone with their families, particularly after I had
been so strongly urging them to stand fast? No, we felt that as long
as we were free to do so, we should keep our family there and continue to stand with our friends."

Eventually, he settled into the routine of prison life, beginning
"to enjoy the period of leisurely contemplation and prayer." He
had a calling while in prison: "prayer—hard, persistent, interces-
sory prayer—was my work." He wrote hymns on the walls. He took
encouragement from those whose bodies were broken but whose
spirit was untouched. Again he was offered the opportunity of release, if he promised to return to America, and again he confound-
ed his interrogators: "As far as my own personal comfort is
concerned, I would like to return to the United States. But as a
missionary I believe that God sent me to this country, and I *want*
to be where I'm supposed to be. No, I do not *want* to go back to
America."

Eventually he was released, on December 5, 1941, after forty-
five days of captivity. He immediately began to pack for the States,
reluctantly accepting deportation. But the attack on Pearl Harbor
occurred two days later, and Japan and America were at war. Hunt
was arrested again and sent to a concentration camp.

Unlike his previous experience, Hunt found himself psycho-
logically unprepared for his second imprisonment: it seemed less
for the cause of the gospel than for the politics of war. Anticipating
harsher treatment and possibly torture, he grew weak and sick from
semi-starvation. As inmates from cells around him were dying,
Hunt had every expectation to be among them. One day he saw a
friend outside his prison window. When he had last seen him,
Choi Han Gee had gone insane in jail. But now he was remarkably
recovered, and he discreetly signaled to Hunt that he and the
church were praying for him. It was a joyful sight for Hunt, more
than repaying him, he said, for all his suffering. Finally, six months
after his arrest, he was released as part of a prisoner exchange. Despite his desire to stay in the country, the government ordered that
he be deported.

Immediately after the war, Hunt went to Korea to serve on the
faculty of the new Korean Seminary in Pusan. He found there a na-

tion characterized by both political and religious confusion. The church was divided by the 38th parallel, the post-war settlement that separated Korea into Soviet and American occupation zones. Hunt felt that the confused state of the country provided a real opening for an active missionary program.

But Hunt's sufferings did not end with his release from captivity. In some respects, his most difficult days lay ahead. He faced ecclesiastical, theological, and cultural struggles similar to those in the United States which had brought the OPC into existence. Probably the greatest difficulty Hunt faced during these years was having to address the sin of shrine worship in the Korean church. Most of the Presbyterian church's leaders had compromised during the period of Japanese persecution. The post-war church was divided on how to treat those who had renounced professions of faith for acceptance by the government. Many church leaders sought to excuse this sin, following the path of modernist indifferentism. Others argued that such believers should be disciplined by denying them fellowship within the church, even those who had demonstrated repentance. Hunt joined those who urged reconciliation through repentance and discipline.

Unfortunately, the general assembly was controlled by the liberals, including those who took a compromising attitude on the shrine issue. Sympathizers to Hunt remained in Pusan Presbytery. To reform the church, they labored to train committed pastors at the seminary in which Hunt taught. At first the general assembly gave official recognition to this seminary, yet it told the presbytery at Pusan to have nothing to do with Hunt and the missionaries associated with him. It was privately alleged that Hunt belonged to a heretical group. On some occasions he was prevented from scheduled preaching opportunities before groups by what he called "sheer mob methods." By 1949 the difference became so great that two competing presbyteries had emerged in Pusan—one conservative and one liberal. Finally, in 1951 the general assembly refused to recognize the conservative presbytery, in effect excommunicating its members from the denomination. As a result, a new conservative Presbyterian denomination was established.

The most painful part of this experience for Hunt was the spiritual bankruptcy of the American missionaries from mainline churches. These modernists counseled the Korean church to receive back into the church those who had submitted to the government and participated in shrine worship during the war. Hunt described this as a betrayal of trust, far more damaging than the Korean sufferings of two wars. "So-called Christian leaders from America," Hunt lamented, "helped to snatch the Bible from the hands of the Korean Christians. People representing the very denominations which first preached the Word of God in Korea are now undermining the authority of that word."

Throughout these trials Hunt shared in the sufferings with the Korean church. He was deeply respected as a man of faultless integrity. Through his sensitivity to the Koreans, Hunt fostered a close theological relationship between the OPC and conservative Presbyterianism in Korea. It should be added that in the midst of these struggles Hunt resumed his energetic work of itinerating great distances for preaching and other assignments, without the assistance of associates on the field. This pace would eventually take its toll. Overwhelmed by his workload and the tragedies he witnessed as the Korean War broke out, Hunt suffered a breakdown in 1950. The Committee on Foreign Missions arranged for an immediate furlough during which he made a complete recovery. After the end of the Korean War in 1953 he returned to Korea, cementing the ties between the OPC and the conservative churches in that country.

The link that Hunt established was soon strengthened when others joined him in the mission. Ted Hard arrived in 1954, Boyce Spooner in 1956, and Harvie Conn in 1960, together with their families. These and other OP missionaries have contributed to the growth of the church in Korea in several ways. For example, they have been active in church planting but in a manner consistent with the philosophy of the Foreign Missions Committee: namely, that the mission always worked with established indigenous denominations. Hunt lamented the failure of many evangelical missions to exhibit a "church consciousness" and helped to set the OP effort in Korea on a course committed to the church and good church order.

Other important contributions by the OPC to the church in Korea were in the areas of education, literature translation, and leadership training—critical areas for the rapidly growing church. These contributions helped the church to face the threat of modernism and the cults. Mormons and Jehovah's Witnesses, for example, were active and rapidly gaining adherents. Hunt personally believed that his most important work was to help Koreans in evaluating these religious movements, understanding their backgrounds and dangers.

In recent years the Korean church has matured to the point where it is a "sending church," commissioning missionaries to serve in foreign countries. Under the direction of Young Son, an OP missionary, the Missionary Training Institute of Seoul has trained over 350 Koreans who have gone on to serve in over fifty countries. These and the vital witness of Korean Presbyterianism are fruit of the OPC's work in the Orient and the faithful labors of missionaries like Bruce Hunt.

Japan

At the same time that the Foreign Missions Committee commissioned Hunt to serve in Korea, it also sent out other missionaries to the Orient. In 1938, the year of the committee's founding, Malcolm Frehn and Heber McIlwaine arrived in Japan and began work in a country whose constitution guaranteed religious freedom. But that freedom came increasingly under attack. In 1940, as the political tensions which would erupt in World War II escalated, the government demanded that all support for foreign missions be stopped. It also pressured all of the various Christian denominations to form one United Church of Japan (*Kyodan*). At the same time, following its policy in Korea, the Japanese government ordered the church to institute the practice of shrine worship. And as was the case in Korea, the edict had two results: the persecution of the faithful who disobeyed the government and compromise by many of the church leaders. The escalation of war forced Frehn and McIlwaine to return to the United States in 1941.

After the war and with the victory of the Allied Forces, General Douglas MacArthur abolished the Religions Law of the Empire and restored religious freedom to Japan. But the modernists who dominated the United Church of Japan wanted to preserve the union, largely as a face-saving effort to demonstrate that the church had retained its autonomy and integrity. This left conservatives with no choice but to form a new denomination, which

they did in 1946 with the founding of the Reformed Church in Japan. Adopting the Westminster Confession as its doctrinal standard, the new church embraced the Reformed faith in its founding
declaration: "Today, as one branch of this glorious historic Reformed church that desires to be truly ecumenical and orthodox,
our Reformed Church of Christ in Japan has been constituted by
the Japanese in Japan, and we cannot but give thanks that this
church has come to be founded, as through the deep mercy and
leading of God. . . . The hope of the world is in the God of Calvinism."

Because the Reformed Church in Japan was so small at its
founding—the church had only eight churches and about two
hundred members—it welcomed the assistance of foreign missionaries. Leaders of the OPC's Committee on Foreign Missions were
immensely encouraged by these developments and reopened the
denomination's Japan mission, sending in 1951 McIlwaine and
George Uomoto, together with their families. Their tasks included
literature distribution and radio work, but mostly the mission set
out to engage in regular, continual preaching and teaching within
and alongside the indigenous church. This patient work has grown
for four decades, to the point where Japan now has the highest
concentration of OP missionaries in the world.

But the work has met with more intense cultural resistance
than any other OP mission. Less than one percent of the Japanese
population is Christian. Christianity raises deep Japanese suspi-
cions about Western imperialism. Many Japanese are eclectic in
their religious practices and are averse to a faith that makes exclusive claims on behalf of a personal God. Family ties are close, and
children are expected to participate in ancestor worship; those
who convert face serious opposition from their families. Nevertheless, the Reformed Church in Japan has experienced slow and
steady growth. By the time of the church's twentieth anniversary
in 1966, it had sixty-five churches and over four thousand members, another sign of God's rich blessing upon the patient work of
solid Reformed witness. More recent statistics, approximately
ninety congregations and six thousand members, again testify to
the slow but nonetheless steady growth of the Reformed faith in
Japan.

Taiwan

The OP mission to Taiwan, as in the case of Korea and Japan, was conditioned by events, particularly political developments, outside the church's control. In 1948 the communist revolution in China had forced Chiang Kai-shek to flee the mainland for Taiwan, where he established his government. Chiang's exile both closed and opened doors for OP missionaries. In his eagerness to cultivate Western connections (especially military support), Chiang invited American missionaries to Taiwan. In response, the OPC Committee on Foreign Missions sent Egbert Andrews and the Rev. and Mrs. Richard Gaffin, who had worked in mainland China before World War II, thus relocating the Chinese mission in Taiwan.

Eventually, two million Mandarin-speaking refugees migrated with Chiang from the mainland after the revolution. But the majority of the natives did not look favorably on Chiang's rule. Especially unpopular was his decision to introduce Mandarin as the national language over the native tongue, Taiwanese. Strong prejudice and persecution extended in both directions, forcing difficult decisions upon the OP mission. Should it minister in Mandarin to younger people (who were learning Mandarin in school) and in the more urban settings, or in Taiwanese to the generally older, poorer, and more rural population? Should the church's Mandarin-speaking missionaries learn a new language? Should they focus on refugees from the mainland in anticipation of a return to a liberated China? Would a Mandarin-speaking mission indicate support for the unpopular ruling government and compromise its ability to reach the native? Complicating the issue was the presence of other language groups, including the Hokka, one-half million strong, who spoke an entirely different language.

The Taiwan mission debated these issues passionately, since the ways in which Chiang's rule divided the island threatened also to divide the mission itself. Unlike the missions in Korea and Japan, no clear sense of unified mission goals emerged in the OPC work. In the end, the missionaries determined it was best to operate in a decentralized manner, and established, in effect, three different fields. Egbert Andrews (whose wife Betty, a Christian Reformed missionary, joined him when they married in 1957) worked among the Taiwanese in Taipei and Kaohsiung. John Johnston (who arrived in 1954) worked largely in Hsin Chu among the Hokkas, and the Gaffins served in Taichung among the Mandarin-speaking population.

At first the mission worked alongside the Taiwanese Presbyterian Church. Unlike its Korean and Japanese counterparts, this church was regarded as fairly stable immediately after World War II. Yet it had no distinctively Reformed confessional statement, and many of its younger ministers, trained in mainline American seminaries, brought neo-orthodoxy and liberalism into the church. Eventually the Taiwanese church joined the World Council of Churches and ordained women to special office. In response to the church's slow doctrinal decline, the Reformed Presbyterian Church in Taiwan was formed in 1971, assisted by the OP mission, along with missionaries from Korea and New Zealand, representatives of the Reformed Presbyterian Church, Evangelical Synod, and the Christian Reformed Church.

Political tensions resurfaced in the late 1970s when the United States government cut off diplomatic relations with Taiwan and officially recognized the communist government in mainland China. Anti-American rioting threatened the safety of the missionaries, again posing difficult questions for the mission. Could they labor effectively without an American embassy? Would they leave if the Chinese invaded? In effect, the OP mission to Taiwan ended up wrestling with questions very similar to those which Bruce Hunt had encountered three decades earlier in Korea. If the missionaries left, what message would such an action communicate to believers who were undergoing profound suffering and persecution? Providentially, the fears of the mission were not realized, as the political situation stabilized. But the problems which politics posed to the OP work in Taiwan highlighted the tremendous barriers that modern missions face. These problems also underscore the missionaries' utter dependence upon God for spiritual harvest and physical safety.

Conclusion

The history of the OPC's missions to the Orient is, in a sense, three very different stories: encouraging harvest in Korea, slow

growth in Japan, and struggles amid the political and cultural up-
heavals in Taiwan. Yet there are similarities as well. To a remarkable extent, all three fields paralleled the story of American
Presbyterianism a generation earlier. Modernism crept into the
churches, and ministers faithful to the gospel were attacked or
forced out of the pulpit. New denominations were formed, evidence of the faithful remnant who sought to perpetuate a true Reformed and Presbyterian witness. Like J. Gresham Machen, many
of the OPC's missionaries in the Orient were accused of legalism,
of dead orthodoxy, and of splitting the church. In fact, Bruce Hunt
was called the leader of the "Machen sect" and a "heretic" because
he had been disciplined by the PCUSA. Many also experienced
the loneliness of ecclesiastical isolation. But by living through the
struggles that led to the founding of the OPC, Hunt, Gaffin, McIlwaine, and others were prepared to persevere through those struggles on the mission field, and to guide the Korean, Japanese, and
Taiwanese Christians through them.

The OPC not only served these churches through the missionaries who went to Korea, Japan, and Taiwan, but professors at
Westminster Seminary such as John Murray, Cornelius Van Til,
Ned Stonehouse, and E. J. Young, all active OP churchmen, were
very helpful in the establishment and sustenance of Christian witnesses in these missions. These faculty members not only trained
leaders—some of whom actually came from the Orient to study at
Westminster—for work in these foreign churches, but through
their commitment to Scripture and the Westminster Confession
they provided useful tools for ministers and missionaries who confronted imposing traditions such as Buddhism and Confucianism.

Finally, the cultural disenfranchisement which the OPC had
experienced in the United States prepared its missionaries well for
the difficult cross-cultural work of propagating the faith in hostile
environments. As OP missionaries pursued the challenge of com-
municating the gospel of God's salvation in Christ in different cultures, they adapted their message to foreign audiences in ways that
neither exported Western lifestyles nor embraced cultural relativism. The infallible Word of God was their rule for faith and practice, and the theology of the Westminster Confession of Faith was
their banner, not because it was Western but because it was biblical. In the spirit of Machen, they proclaimed a timeless truth that
transcends all cultures.

6
Eritrea

"IT IS ALL OVER." Those were the words Karl Dortzbach used on June 18, 1974, to describe the work of the American Evangelical Mission of the Orthodox Presbyterian Church in Eritrea. They were very discouraging and shocking words for those who supported the OPC's mission efforts in Eritrea and were earnestly hoping for some good news. Yet Dortzbach had good reason for such an alarming assessment. His pregnant wife, Debbie, a nurse at the mission's Compassion of Jesus Hospital, had been kidnapped and was now held hostage by the Eritrean Liberation Front. She was a captive in the escalating animosities between the Ethiopian government and guerrilla forces seeking the independence of the Eritrean province.

The most recent communication from Debbie Dortzbach's captors only reinforced her husband's pessimism. In repeated letters the kidnappers demanded a ransom for the safe return of their hostage. At first they had demanded $75,000 plus an additional $10,000 in medical and other supplies. Later, the amount was reduced to $12,500. Each time Karl steadfastly refused, not in an effort to obtain a better price, but because he was following the official guidelines of the OPC. Twenty years earlier, the Committee on Foreign Missions had established the policy that no ransom was to be paid. "Under no circumstances," the committee insisted, "may moneys . . . be used for the ransom of any of the missionary family." In the case of the Dortzbachs it was not simply that the committee would not overturn a well-established principle of foreign missions; the OPC's austere missions budget did not have sufficient funds for even the smaller ransom figure.

For these reasons it now seemed that Debbie would share the fate of her fellow missionary nurse, Anna Strikwerda, who, just a few weeks earlier on May 27th, had been brutally murdered during a raid on the missionary hospital where she and the Dortzbachs worked. Despite several frustrating efforts to negotiate through intermediaries, the Eritrean Liberation Front remained adamant. In a letter dated June 14, the kidnappers warned that the mission must assume responsibility for its refusal to pay the ransom. Karl Dortzbach was sure that this letter sealed the fate of his wife and unborn child. He would later describe his ambivalent emotions during that long day spent in prayer: "Confusion and uncertainty, discouragement and despair, still riddled me; but almost imperceptibly hope inched into my mind—hope in God's power."

On the evening of the 18th another letter arrived with inexplicable and remarkable news. The Eritrean Liberation Front had determined to release Debbie Dortzbach unharmed and without conditions. Four days later she was reunited with her husband and the mission. The ordeal of the 26-day kidnapping, the anguish and hardships encountered, and the peace and comfort in God's gracious provision are recounted by the Dortzbachs in their book, *Kidnapped* (1975). But despite this book's happy ending, Karl Dortzbach's words, "It is all over," settled over the Eritrean mission. The mission would be shut down because of the escalating confrontation between the Eritrean factions.

Would God allow this land to be forsaken for long? Before we answer this question, it would be helpful to take a closer look at the origins of OP mission efforts in Eastern Africa.

Churchly Missions

The founding of the OPC's Committee on Foreign Missions in 1936 marked a radical departure from the missions philosophy that dominated conservative Protestantism, whether evangelical or fundamentalist, throughout the first half of the twentieth century. While conservatives had generally supported a variety of missionary organizations which were non-denominational, dispensationalist, Arminian in theology, and free from ecclesiastical oversight, the OPC's work was probably the only effort in foreign missions which explicitly rejected theological modernism and at the same time championed Calvinist theology, a high view of special office, and the necessity of connections to and dependence upon a supporting denomination. The OPC, true to the tradition of Old School Presbyterianism, testified to the belief that missions and evangelism were ministries reserved strictly for the church. According to this perspective, the task of proclaiming the gospel is to be carried out only by ordained ministers and evangelists, who depend upon the church for oversight, edification, and financial support.

The Presbyterian polity of OP missions has prevented the denomination from repeating some of the errors that have plagued evangelical missions. Unlike evangelical missions agencies which lack ecclesiastical oversight and are often subject to the sometimes capricious preferences of powerful personalities, OP missionaries are bound by the same set of theological standards which the church sets for its ministers.

Another significant blessing which comes from making the church, as opposed to the parachurch, responsible for missionary work is a clear vision of the nature and purpose of missions. The OPC has insisted that Christ ordained the visible church for the proclamation of the gospel and that the church has been uniquely gifted for this task. This understanding of the gospel and of the church has always functioned as a check upon the temptation to enlarge the work of the missions beyond the proclamation of the Word of God. Only in rare cases, as in the dire circumstances of Northeast Africa, has the OPC included other activities. And this feature of the OPC's missions has set the denomination apart from evangelical missions agencies which, because of a low view of the church and special office, have ironically repeated the errors of mainline missions. Not only have evangelical missions included activities common to human society in the work of foreign missions, but the blurring of the lines between saving and common grace, or between special and general revelation, has once again raised questions in some evangelical missions circles about the uniqueness of the Christian mission and ultimately about the nature of salvation.

Also, unlike evangelical missions which have sent out large numbers of missionaries to convert as many as possible and as soon as possible because of the imminence of Christ's return (a motive stemming directly from the teachings of dispensational premillennialism), the OPC has been committed to the more ordinary and deliberate work of establishing churches which will continue to minister God's Word to many generations of believers. To be sure, the OPC shares the zeal of evangelicals to spread the good news of God's grace in Christ and convert the elect. This is, after all, *the* biblical mandate for missions. But the church has been reluctant to abandon the means God ordained for reaching the lost, and it has not seen conversion as the sole end of missions. Rather, its strategy in foreign missions differs little from its aims at home. The goal of foreign missions has been to establish churches committed to Reformed theology and faithful to Presbyterian polity. This goal is the result of the OPC's belief that foreign missionaries, like American pastors, are to proclaim the whole counsel of God, not merely the bare bones of the gospel. For this reason, the OPC has taken seriously Christ's command in the Great Commission to make disciples and baptize them. This work involves missionary efforts committed to the long haul.

As is also evident in the case of OP missions to Eritrea, however, this commitment does not come without exacting a high price. Indeed, the OPC's dedication to the slow and deliberate labor of establishing churches and instructing believers in the wonderful truths of the Reformed faith has often met, as in the case of the Dortzbachs, with what have appeared to be overwhelming difficulties. But despite the trials which OP missionaries have endured, God has richly blessed the work in Africa because he is faithful to his promises.

"A Hot, Barren, Rocky, Mohammedan Field"

In April of 1941, while the war in the Pacific theater was forcing OP missionaries in Japan, China, and Manchuria to return home, the British liberated the nation of Ethiopia from the Italians when they captured the capital, Addis Ababa, from Mussolini's forces. For Clarence Duff, this provided an opportunity to return to the land where he had labored for eleven years with the Sudan

Interior Mission (SIM). Serving at the time as an OP home missionary in Colorado, Duff wrote to the Committee on Foreign Missions proposing that it consider a work in Africa. The committee
responded enthusiastically to Duff's proposal, and in 1943 Duff
traveled alone to Africa to survey the field and to gain a permit of
entry in Ethiopia.

Duff's overtures to the Committee on Foreign Missions signaled a major shift in his missionary career. In leaving the Sudan
Interior Mission for the OPC, Duff left one of the most prominent
of the evangelical "faith missions" agencies (such as China Inland
Mission or Africa Inland Mission) that had started around the turn
of the twentieth century. These parachurch agencies were convinced that the task of missions was more efficiently conducted
outside of the restraints of denominational control. Staff members
were characteristically lay people, trained at dispensational
schools such as Moody Bible Institute or Philadelphia College of
the Bible, and sent to the mission field generally without seminary
training. Convinced that the time was short before the return of
Jesus, and urged on by a revivalist mentality that sought to win decisions for Christ, evangelical faith missions placed a strong priority on massive evangelistic campaigns to reach the lost. Faith
missions were quick to use the latest in technology, such as radio
and airplanes, but reluctant to reflect carefully on the nature and
purpose of the missionary task. All of these characteristics—the
dramatic urgency of its task, the downplaying of potentially divisive doctrines, and the appeal of a technique-oriented ministry—
served to win for faith missions large support from fundamentalists
and evangelicals.

Formed in 1893, SIM expanded rapidly in the first two decades
of the twentieth century, counting five hundred missionaries on its
rolls by 1945. But Clarence Duff would not be found on those lists.
When he returned to the United States in 1938, Duff immediately
left the PCUSA for the OPC, along with his wife, Dorothea,
whom he had met and married on the mission field. Although he
left many friends at SIM, he chose the less popular route of ecclesiastical missions, fully committed to the cause of the young
church.

But the path he chose would prove immediately to be a difficult one. Duff's initial plans to obtain a permit of entry to return

to Ethiopia met with formidable resistance. In a letter to Foreign Missions general secretary Robert Marsden, he outlined his problems: "The fact that I am representing a new organization may make it more difficult. The policy of the Ethiopian government is to allow entry only of personnel of established societies."

Instead, Duff determined to go to Eritrea, which at the time was under the friendlier rule of the British Military Administration. Through previous work Duff had established friendships with other missionary societies which proved helpful in starting the Eritrean work. Although Marsden had urged Duff to make every effort to enter Ethiopia, he sensed the frustration of the denomination because of the number of delays that Duff experienced, and so he agreed with Duff's decision to press on in Eritrea. It was increasingly evident that Eritrea held greater promise for the establishment of a church.

Duff described the challenge before him in a letter to Marsden in 1944: "The difficulties are rather staggering—climate, modern prejudice, terrifically rugged terrain in the mountainous parts, difficult language or languages, semi-nomadic habits of many of the people." The work was far different from his previous missions experience. He called it a "hot, barren, rocky, Mohammedan field" that contrasted sharply with the "green mountains and flowing springs" of southern Ethiopia, and he likened Eritrea's "extreme heat, scorching winds, and sudden floods" to Israel's experience in the wilderness.

Yet in that forbidding environment a mission grew. As Duff surveyed the field, he saw the need for many workers and, in effect, two missions—one to the Ethiopic Coptic church and another to the Muslims. In 1944 Charles Stanton arrived; later his wife Fern joined him, and they served until 1949. Francis and Arlena Mahaffy came a year later and would serve there until 1968. The fact that these missionaries and their families traveled to Africa under the perilous conditions of a world war encouraged Duff in the denomination's commitment to the Great Commission.

The mission needed long periods of laborious plowing before it began to reap any significant fruit. Several different languages had to be learned and relationships of trust had to be established. Several times the mission was frustrated by painful defections of individuals who had made what seemed were genuine professions of faith. The persecution and ostracism faced by new converts were harsh. Ten years would pass before the mission would realize the spiritual harvest of new believers. Gradually, there were encouraging results from their longer-term perseverance. "As the years pass," wrote Duff, "evidence comes from here and there that some of the good seed thought to have been wasted has much later, often in some other part of the country, borne good fruit."

As the mission developed, it confronted two issues that engaged the young church at large as it developed basic principles of foreign missions. The first was the issue of control of the mission churches and the second was the role of medicine on the mission field.

The Goal of the Mission: Indigenous Churches

In a 1950 article in the *Presbyterian Guardian*, Clarence Duff reflected at some length on the goal of the young new mission. He noted how, historically, many other missions faced difficulties from excessive control by the sponsoring American church. He compared traditional missions with a new plan that he found encouraging. The old plan consisted of "foreign support, foreign affiliation, and foreign control." The new plan consisted of "native finance, native affiliation, and native control." The goal of missions, he asserted, was truly Presbyterian native churches: "the only hope of discipling all nations is through native churches in each country." He found biblical precedent for this in the missionary efforts of the apostles. Further, the limited resources of the OPC demanded that the church conduct its missions program most efficiently and not waste any energy or means.

Duff anticipated some resistance to his idea. Could a newly established church take responsibility for its government, support, and growth? Could it provide discipline and mature elders? Duff was confident that it could. In fact, he argued that native Christians were in a better position to exercise discipline, and that their rule was likely to be more effective. The mission developed a three-fold strategy: 1) thorough and widespread evangelism, 2) careful instruction of all converts, and 3) the ordination of elders.

This thinking lay behind the name for the mission, the American Evangelical Mission of the Orthodox Presbyterian Church.

All three elements of the name were carefully chosen. "American" usefully capitalized on the popularity of America among the Eritreans. "Evangelical" set the mission off from Roman Catholic missions or Coptic churches, although Duff recognized the imprecision of the name: "no doubt much additional meaning can and ought to be put into the word through instruction." Finally, "Mission" properly distinguished it from the church, which would be established by natives. "Let the mission be foreign," Duff wrote, "but let the church be native." Not only was Duff's reasoning biblical, its stress on local control wisely anticipated the anti-Western attitudes of the decolonization movement that characterized post-World War II Africa.

Another consequence of Duff's mission philosophy—one that has characterized the work of the OPC in general—was that the Eritrean mission would support rigorous educational work. Evangelism was not enough. The emerging church had to be strengthened through a program of Christian education, thus heeding Christ's command in the Great Commission to make disciples. The translation and publishing of solid Christian literature was always a priority in the mission. Francis Mahaffy translated portions of the New Testament into the Saho language and produced over a dozen booklets and tracts in that language. Working among the Coptics, Herbert Bird worked on Bible and catechism translation into the Tigrinya language.

The Means of the Mission: Ministry of Mercy

In the same 1950 article in the *Presbyterian Guardian*, Duff raised the question about the role of medical work in foreign missions: "Is it merely an auxiliary to evangelism, an attraction to get people to listen to the gospel? Or does it have a sphere of its own, in manifesting the compassion of Christ through the ministry of healing?" These were not merely hypothetical questions for Duff. From the outset of the work in Eritrea, the Duffs were overwhelmed by the country's staggering medical needs. The little ministry of mercy that they could provide opened many doors for gospel witness. By 1948 Duff appealed for help in a letter to Robert Marsden. "We are more than ever convinced," Duff wrote, "that a trained nurse would find a most profitable field of work here in

Ghinda. Furthermore, if we do not soon have someone who is capable of doing medical work in a proper manner, I don't know what we shall do."

The Duffs and the Mahaffys continued to provide medical care, and by 1952 they were treating up to one hundred patients a day. The urgency of the situation was highlighted in the *Orthodox Presbyterian Messenger*: "The pitiful need for medical help has surrounded the missionaries on every hand and in spite of their lack of special training they have helped [patients] in their need as they have been able to do so." Meanwhile, the government established higher qualifications for medical workers, and unlicensed workers were subject to malpractice prosecution. The mission was convinced that it had to recruit trained and licensed medical missionaries.

In response to these needs, a nurse arrived in 1949 but she soon left, unable to adjust to the mission field. Again in 1956 a team of English nurses arrived from the Red Sea Mission but their help proved to be temporary. They served in the Ghinda clinic only until 1959. In the 1960s, the Committee on Foreign Missions was finally able to appoint and send doctors to the field. In 1964 Dr. John Den Hartog arrived in Eritrea and the following year Dr. Lyle Nilson, along with several nurses, completed the medical team. In that same year the committee voted to construct a small, fifty-bed hospital in Ghinda. Much of the cost of the hospital was actually subsidized by three Reformed Church in America congregations in Michigan and Iowa.

The decision to build a hospital finally forced the OPC to address the questions Duff had raised in 1950 about the propriety of medical missions. Is medicine part of the Great Commission and is there biblical warrant for the church *as the church* to practice medicine? Or is medicine, as part of the cultural mandate, something outside the church's authority which should be left to individual Christians in the course of their vocational responsibilities?

In 1963 the general assembly asked the Committee on Foreign Missions to report on the scriptural principles for the ministry of mercy in the church at the next assembly. That report argued that "the Scriptures not only sanction or permit medical missionary work but also require it under conditions of need." It went on to argue that Jesus expressed concern for both the healing of the body and the soul, and that the continuing church should follow his example of compassion for both.

The report did not satisfy one member of the Foreign Missions Committee, Meredith Kline, then a professor of Old Testament at Westminster Seminary. In his minority report, Kline claimed that the committee violated the principle of "sphere sovereignty," which held that different social structures had separate spheres or areas of responsibility. No social institution should perform the work appointed for another. Specifically, Kline argued, the church could not claim for itself tasks that fall in the sphere of general human culture (such as medical work). Instead, the clear teaching of Scripture was that the church should restrict itself to the ecclesiastical functions of the preaching of the gospel and the administration of the sacraments.

Herbert Bird responded to Kline on behalf of the majority of the committee. Bird first noted the difficulty that affluent Western cultures have in appreciating the value of mercy ministries in underdeveloped countries. Eritrea was not a place "where the pure teaching of the Word will not be complicated by the demands of human wretchedness." Bird also agreed in general with the principle of sphere sovereignty, but he felt that Kline drew too fine a distinction between the church's task in carrying out the Great Commission and individual Christian responsibility in pursuing the cultural mandate. Could the church ever engage in cultural activities? Bird thought Kline's "never!" was too extreme. Instead, a balanced biblical response was "hardly ever." Here Bird compared the work of medicine and translation. The medical missionary, he argued, is no less engaged in cultural activities than the missionary linguist who commits an unwritten language to writing in order to translate the Bible. His conclusion—that "a ministry of mercy is a valid expression of Christian concern by the church as church"—convinced the 1964 Assembly, which approved the construction of the mission hospital.

Defeat or Bright Promise?

Despite efforts to establish indigenous churches and the construction and administration of a small hospital, the OPC had no control over the political turmoil that continued to torment the nation of Eritrea. Indeed, the murder of Anna Strikwerda, the first martyr of the OPC, and the kidnapping of Debbie Dortzbach made clear just how much the work in Eritrea was captive to the forces of political intrigue. Consequently, the surprising release of Mrs. Dortzbach in 1974 did not end the dangers to the Eritrean mission. The trauma of war continued to escalate as Marxist rebels sought control of the government. During the civil war, OP missionaries endured the terror of frequent local shootings and exploding land mines. Finally, in 1976 Osman Adem, a dedicated worker in the hospital, was seized and never seen alive again. Immediately, the mission and the hospital closed, ending thirty-two years of service. The remaining missionaries returned to the United States.

No doubt the departing missionaries, along with the home church hearing the news, were tempted to repeat Karl Dortzbach's words, "It is all over." Clarence Duff, now in retirement, reflected on the grim events that led to the closing of the hospital in the *Presbyterian Guardian*: "Is this latest development to spell defeat, or is there promise of a bright outcome? On the surface it must surely seem like defeat. But need it be so?"

Despite the appearance of defeat, the goal of the mission had been accomplished, namely, the planting of an indigenous church. "God has indeed called out a little church in Eritrea through the labors of these missionaries," Duff wrote. "I do not believe he is about to abandon this branch of the Living Vine. But neither must we! We must remember her! We must daily remind the Lord of his promise to his church, to every true congregation of his people." There were small groups of believers in Ghinda and surrounding villages, and three strong leaders who had been ordained as elders.

And the work was not finished, Duff insisted. The Eritrean mission of the OPC would need to continue. "As long as present conditions in Eritrea continue, it may not be wise or even possible to have direct communications with the church there. But by way of the throne of grace in heaven we can uphold her and have a mighty influence on her for blessing. The answer to our question, 'Defeat or bright promise?' may depend in large measure on our home churches. Are we going to acquiesce in what appears to be sad defeat for the cause of Christ? Or will we rise up in the power of the Holy Spirit to plead God's promises and to claim victory in Christ's name? It can make all the difference!" Duff exhorted the church to remain hopeful in the promises of God. He reminded them that God would glorify himself in these events that he was controlling. There was no cause for despair.

New Hope in Eritrea

It has been nearly two decades since the closing of the Eritrean mission and hospital, but the work of OP missions there has not ended. In 1991 the thirty-year war ended when Eritrea finally gained its independence from Ethiopia. Now with one of the most stable of African governments, Eritrea has recently been reopened for OP missionary work. In 1992 a contingent from the Committee on Foreign Missions returned to the hospital that the OPC still owned. The team was shocked at the effects of the war, from the bombed-out hospital to the more than fifty thousand orphans produced by the conflict. The needs were more desperate than ever. Still, they were encouraged by the faith of old friends—the indigenous church had survived.

With the promise of religious freedom from the new government, Don and Jeanette Taws, who served from 1958 to 1961, returned to the field for three years to reestablish the mission. Recently the church sent Charles and Rhonda Telfer and Steve and Jane Miller, who have been astounded by the hunger for the gospel, as Bible studies and worship services meet in overflowing rooms. The Foreign Missions Committee is now exploring the feasibility of reopening medical work.

God has marvelously answered the prayers of the church since the time when Clarence Duff began the mission to Eritrea in 1943. He continued to answer the prayers of the church throughout the Dortzbachs' ordeal. And he answered the prayers of the church by calling the Tawses and Telfers to reopen the mission. As Foreign Missions general secretary Mark Bube recently wrote while reviewing the history of the work in Eritrea, "It is reassuring to know that our God does not change and that he remains ever faithful to his promises. Yes, our God does hear and answer the prayers of his children. To him be the glory!"

To be sure, the story of the OPC's mission efforts in other parts of the world lacks the drama and political intrigue of the work in Eritrea. Yet, the Eritrean mission does testify to the denomination's ongoing commitment to spreading the good news of the gospel around the world, no matter how difficult or dangerous. The OPC was conceived during controversies over the nature and task of missions, and its persistent labors, at home and abroad, demonstrate the church's deep and abiding concern for the work of evangelism. By God's grace it shall continue to proclaim the gospel of sovereign redemption to the ends of the earth.

PART THREE
ECUMENICITY

The OPC WAS BORN in the midst of controversy. As we noted earlier, J. Gresham Machen wrote privately to one fellow minister that the greatest qualification for being a part of the conservative Presbyterian movement was that he "be a fighter." In fact, Machen thought the cause of the OPC would "die of inaction" unless pastors and elders kept up the "ecclesiastical fight."

These are not the sentiments we associate with ecumenicity, the effort to make visible the unity of the body of Christ. Machen's words may strike readers today, as they did his contemporaries in the mainline Presbyterian Church, as narrow, intolerant, and mean—the exact opposite of those characteristics necessary for seeking closer ties between the various Christian communions. And it cannot be denied that Machen opposed the broad church policies which dominated American Protestantism during his life. But these policies which seemed to display tolerance and love, as he argued, actually stemmed from thorough-going indifference to the teachings of the Bible and the claims of the Westminster Confession.

Thus, from its inception the OPC has had the reputation of being anti-ecumenical. But this reputation has been based upon a false understanding of ecumenicity. The OPC has clearly opposed the kind of ecumenical relations favored by liberal Protestantism (and sometimes by evangelicalism), but it does possess a remarkable record of seeking fraternal relations with Presbyterian and Reformed bodies around the world. The OPC, as it turns out, has not been anti-ecumenical but rather has pursued ecumenicity for very different reasons from those of mainline Protestantism. It has sought fellowship with other communions not out of sentimental and vague ideals of good will and Christian brotherhood, but rather on the basis of its commitment to the Reformed faith. As Machen explained,

> We do not risk losing our Christian fellowship with our true brethren in other communions if we hold honestly to our ordination

pledge. Let us hold to it honestly; and let us not abandon in the interests of any vague inter-denominationalism or anti-denominationalism, that great system of revealed truth which is taught in holy Scripture and is so gloriously summarized in the Standards of our Church.

The chapters which follow demonstrate how the OPC has carried out this conception of ecumenicity. While its rigorous commitment to the Westminster Standards has often cut the church off (at least on a formal level) from other Protestants in the United States, both evangelicals and liberals, the OPC has consistently held cordial and deep relationships with Presbyterian and Reformed churches in the United States and in other countries. The OPC's ecumenical policies make clear that doctrine or common confession is the basis for unity and fellowship with other Christians. Indeed, what unites the OPC with other churches is not a shared commitment to America's well-being or to world order, as important as social stability is for the proclamation of the gospel. Rather, what unites the church to other Reformed communions is a common confession about the Lord of glory, the riches of God's love in Jesus Christ, and the nature and means of salvation offered in the gospel.

7
The OPC and the New
Evangelicalism

WITH THE DIVISION OF 1937, the OPC signaled that it was
not a fundamentalist church. Though the denomination was born
in the context of combatting modernism, the founders of the OPC
had more in mind than merely fighting liberal theology. Equally
important was the church's Reformed identity. And as the decisions of the first three general assemblies made clear, the OPC was
not merely conservative but resolutely Presbyterian. Indeed, as
Machen had argued many times throughout the fundamentalist
controversy, the surest safeguard against modernism was not some
lowest-common-denominator conservative theology but rather a
deep commitment to Presbyterian faith and practice as revealed in
God's Word.

While many would concede that the OPC is not a fundamentalist church, some might wonder whether it would be fair to describe the denomination as evangelical. After all, evangelical
Christianity is also conservative theologically (i.e., suspicious of
liberal Protestantism) and avoids the excesses of fundamentalism.
Also, evangelicals tend to be conservative politically and socially,
a characteristic that entails concerns about a number of social
problems that also trouble Orthodox Presbyterians.

Much of the debate about whether the OPC is evangelical de-
pends upon one's definition of evangelicalism. The origins of the
word "evangelical" date back to the Protestant Reformation when
followers of Martin Luther designated themselves evangelical because they believed they had rediscovered the gospel (*euangelion*).
To this day, Lutheran churches in Germany are still known as

evangelical. In the United States, the evangelical label has had less to do with denominations or churches than with revivalism, itinerant evangelists, and the recounting of one's conversion experience. Despite the Calvinistic theology which inspired the eighteenth-century revivals of George Whitefield and Jonathan Edwards, the pattern of itinerant preaching and mass meetings that was set into motion during the First Great Awakening stamped American evangelicalism indelibly with its distinctive style. With the revivals of Charles Finney at the time of the Second Great Awakening, learning, tradition, formality, and ordination took a back seat to the sovereignty of the audience, charismatic leadership, and pragmatic know-how.

But while the evangelical tradition in America has such a long history, contemporary evangelicalism has a considerably narrower focus. The fundamentalist controversy of the 1920s severed the ties that bound mainstream Protestantism and spawned a few new denominations, numerous independent congregations, and a host of parachurch organizations that in the 1940s came together to constitute the movement we today call evangelicalism. Interestingly, though the OPC shared many of the aims of this new evangelicalism, it remained organizationally separate as church leaders declined invitations to join what would become the associations of the evangelical establishment. To some evangelicals, the OPC's unwillingness to cooperate with other conservatives was as indicative of folly as it was of pride. But in the light of its Reformed identity, the OPC's coolness toward the new evangelicalism made perfect sense.

The Clark Controversy

Relations between the OPC and other conservative Protestant denominations and organizations was the background for perhaps the greatest theological debate that has ever occurred in the denomination's history. This was the notorious controversy from 1943 to 1948 over the ordination of Gordon H. Clark, who was for much of his career professor of philosophy at Butler University and for a brief time a minister in the OPC. The doctrine at issue specifically was the incomprehensibility of God, or the degree to which men and women know God truly. But the sometimes obscure theological debates at work in this conflict were always bound up with the larger question about the OPC's relationship to the broader evangelical community and the church's Presbyterian identity. Would the church be narrowly Reformed or would it be an important voice in the larger project of restoring Christianity in America? The debates over Clark revealed two different visions for the mission and character of the OPC.

The controversy began in 1943 when Clark sought ordination by the OPC's Presbytery of Philadelphia. From 1936 until 1943, Clark had been professor of philosophy at Wheaton College. J. Oliver Buswell had hired him to teach at the evangelical liberal arts college. But Buswell's involvement in the Presbyterian controversies of the 1930s led college officials to request his resignation as president. And with Buswell gone, Clark's Calvinistic teaching and strong views on predestination found few sympathetic ears. In 1943 the new president of Wheaton College, V. Raymond Edman, asked Clark to resign because his theology was said to undermine the school's commitment to evangelism and missions.

With a view toward teaching at Reformed Episcopal Seminary in Philadelphia, Clark requested ordination from the OPC's Presbytery of Philadelphia. Though he lacked formal theological training, Clark was a gifted philosopher, having earned a Ph.D. in philosophy from the University of Pennsylvania and having authored several textbooks on various aspects of philosophy. He also had a reputation for being a scintillating lecturer who captivated students with his powers of reasoning. Furthermore, Clark had been an active elder in the church, and a frequent contributor to the *Presbyterian Guardian*. Consequently, the Presbytery of Philadelphia waived some of its ordination requirements and proceeded to examine Clark's theological views. While the presbytery voted 15 to 13 to sustain Clark in his candidacy for the ministry, the OPC's Form of Government requires that ministerial candidates be approved by a three-fourths majority. So Clark would have to face another examination by the presbytery, which occurred in July 1944. This time Clark passed. He was licensed to preach and ordained at the same meeting.

What emerged during debates in the presbytery over Clark's views were two different perspectives, very similar to the ones which in 1937 had disrupted the OPC. Those who supported

Clark comprised the party of "American Presbyterianism." After the departure of Carl McIntire and the formation of the Bible Presbyterian Synod, the doctrines of dispensationalism and premillennialism were no longer at issue but other points of contention remained. Those in the Americanist party opposed the leadership which the faculty of Westminster Seminary exerted in the OPC. They blamed such Dutch and Scotch Calvinists as Cornelius Van Til, Ned Stonehouse, and John Murray for giving the church an image of being overly doctrinaire and unnecessarily sectarian. American Presbyterianism, according to Clark's supporters, had always made room for cooperating with Christians who were not Calvinists and promoted such social causes as Prohibition.

Differences between these two points of view came to the surface in an exchange in the *Presbyterian Guardian*. Dr. Edward J. Young, professor of Old Testament at Westminster, in the September 25, 1944 issue asked the question, "Is Arminianism the Gospel?" His answer was a definitive "no!" Young rejected Arminian teaching which gave man the final say in salvation and affirmed the characteristic Calvinistic notion that God alone is sovereign in redemption. To this article Dr. Robert Strong, minister to an OP congregation just outside Philadelphia, replied that Young was guilty of "loose reasoning," argued that many Arminians did in fact preach the gospel, and warned lest the OPC define Christianity only in terms of Calvinism.

As it happened, Strong had stepped in at the beginning of the struggle over Clark's ordination. For at the same time that Strong challenged Young's defense of Calvinism, thirteen members of the Presbytery of Philadelphia objected to Clark's licensure and ordination, led by Ned Stonehouse, Cornelius Van Til, R. B. Kuiper, Paul Woolley, and Edward J. Young. Their complaint pointed out that the proceedings of the July presbytery meeting were irregular and that Clark's theological views should have prevented him from being ordained. Specifically, the complainants objected to Clark's ideas about human knowledge of God. Even though they agreed that God could be known by men and women because of his revelation in Scripture and through the work of the Holy Spirit, they maintained against Clark that such human knowledge is never identical to God's knowledge. Indeed, Clark's opponents believed that Clark came perilously close to denying the qualitative distinction between the knowledge of the Creator and the knowledge of the creature. They also accused Clark of denying the difference between the knowledge of God which believers have as opposed to unbelievers (the effect of regeneration on the intellect), and of holding hyper-Calvinistic views about the relationship between divine sovereignty and human responsibility, and the free offer of the gospel. To his credit, there can be no doubt of Clark's sincerity and zeal to defend the truths of Scripture. But Clark's claim to explain the great mysteries of the Bible appeared to lead to rationalistic qualifications of the very truths he had set out to defend.

Even though Clark was in no respect friendly toward Arminianism, his ordination became part of the larger struggle between the party of American Presbyterianism and the faculty at Westminster Seminary. The Americanists particularly believed that Clark sympathized with their goals. He was also known to oppose key elements in the presuppositional apologetics of Dr. Van Til. Hence, for Americanists in the Presbytery of Philadelphia, defending Clark was a key element in their cause. In fact, Dr. Strong in 1944 went so far as to issue "A Program of Action in the OPC," a plan which involved four specific objectives: 1) the ordination of Gordon H. Clark, 2) affiliation with one of the larger interdenominational fundamentalist associations, 3) an official declaration against the sale and distribution of liquor, and 4) supervision by the OPC of Westminster Seminary and the *Presbyterian Guardian*. Clark's ordination, therefore, was just one facet of a much larger effort to control the denomination.

In response to the complaint filed by opponents of Clark's ordination, the Presbytery of Philadelphia appointed a committee of five, including Clark and Strong. Their task was to reply to Clark's critics. The committee cleared Clark of the charges that he denied the distinction between the Creator and creature, that he held a faulty understanding of regeneration, and that his views on salvation deviated from the theology of the Westminster Confession. In effect, Clark, through the committee, denied all charges, and where the points at issue concerned philosophical differences he held that the Confession of Faith allowed for a diversity of views, especially regarding the nature of human knowledge of God. Clark's response was not merely defensive. He also protested that his critics encouraged agnosticism and skepticism. If we do not know the things God has revealed in the same way as God knows them, he reasoned, then there is no connection between God's and our knowledge and we are left with "unmitigated skepticism." The committee's report received close scrutiny and initiated a lengthy debate. Though it was not adopted by presbytery, it did allow Clark the chance to explain his views.

With the matter unresolved, the Clark controversy came before the General Assembly of 1945 by appeal. This body ruled that the Presbytery of Philadelphia had erred in ordaining Clark, not because of problems in his theology, but because the presbytery had not allowed for sufficient time between Clark's licensure and ordination. The presbytery should not have decided upon Clark's licensure and ordination at the same meeting. Still, the assembly did not overturn Clark's ordination. The general assembly was, however, concerned about the doctrinal problems raised in the Clark affair and appointed a committee to look into this aspect of the debate, thus upholding the OPC's reputation for theological and procedural precision. At the same time that other Protestant churches in America considered how they might best respond to the temporal crises stemming from World War II, the OPC pursued vigorously an issue which must have seemed an extraneous consideration to a world ravaged by war. But the OPC has always viewed questions of grace and eternal salvation as the most weighty of human considerations and has understood that the primary task of the church is to address matters such as this, even if unimportant by the world's standards.

The majority report from the committee appointed by the general assembly to look into the affair sided with Clark. As the reports indicated, part of the problem stemmed from a flawed stenographic record of Clark's examination before presbytery. It was not complete and in many instances communicated inaccuracies. This made the task of figuring out Clark's views extremely difficult. The majority, taking into account the problems of the record, concluded that the complaints against Clark could not be sustained. While committee members may not have cared for some of Clark's expressions and would have asked for further clarification had they been at the exam, they decided that Clark's ideas did not contradict Scripture or the Westminster Standards.

One of the members of the committee appointed by the general assembly was John Murray, professor of systematic theology at Westminster. Until this time he had taken no direct part in the controversy because he belonged to the Presbytery of New York and New England. In comparison with other systematic theologians of his time, Murray was notable, if not unique, for his ability to derive clear doctrinal formulations from careful exegesis, thus showing that the truths of the Reformed faith come straight from Scripture. In the end, Murray was the decisive figure in the Clark controversy. His learned and faithful work in the areas of God's incomprehensibility and the free offer of the gospel made a lasting contribution to twentieth-century Reformed theology.

In the minority report, Murray agreed with the majority in many respects, but was disturbed as much by the presbytery's ordination of Clark as by his views. He did not think that Clark had contradicted the Bible or the Confession, but did believe that the presbytery should not have been satisfied with Clark's answers and should have pushed him for a fuller expression of all his views before approving his candidacy. Murray viewed statements in Clark's answers about the incomprehensibility of God as insufficient, not erroneous. Rather than describing God's incomprehensibility in relation to the various ways that humans receive knowledge about God, Murray wrote, "the incomprehensibility of God should be stated in terms of the transcendent glory and mystery of the being, relations, perfections and counsel of God." In other words, it was not so much that Clark's ideas about the relationship between human and divine knowledge were incorrect, but that Clark's thoughts did not do justice to the majesty and glory of God. Murray sensed that Clark had not given a "satisfactory and unequivocal" expression of the magnitude and mystery of God's glory. Rather than arguing that Clark should not have been ordained, the minority report asked for further examination of Clark before approving him for the ministry.

Both reports, then, typified the OPC's high regard for Reformed confessionalism. The majority believed that as long as a candidate was in agreement with the teaching of Scripture as expressed in the Westminster Confession, he should be licensed and ordained. Murray's minority report, however, reflected the theological convictions at the heart of Reformed theology. As the first answer to the Shorter Catechism states, "Man's chief end is to glorify God and enjoy him forever." Indeed, Calvinist theology begins and ends with God's glory. And because Clark did not unequivocally make the majesty and mystery of God's glory the foundation for theology, Murray, who spoke for other critics of Clark, believed that Clark should be called upon to give a fuller and better expression of his views. This report confirmed what many had suspected, namely, that significant theological matters were at stake. In turn, the General Assembly of 1946 appointed another committee to study and clarify the doctrines of "the incomprehensibility of God, the position of the intellect in reference to other faculties, the relation of divine sovereignty and human responsibility, and the free offer of the gospel."

The new committee, which included Murray and Stonehouse, labored diligently and prepared a report of fifty-four pages that was printed in the Agenda for the 1947 Assembly. But the report never made it to the floor of the general assembly owing to a dramatic turn during the proceedings of the 1947 gathering. The event which absorbed the attention of the delegates was the decision by the Committee on Foreign Missions not to send Floyd E. Hamilton to Korea. A veteran of missionary work in Korea, Hamilton had been invited to return and teach at a seminary. The Committee on Foreign Missions, however, which included John Murray, was unwilling to send Hamilton because of his advocacy and defense of Clark's views.

Thus, the Clark controversy spilled over onto other aspects of the OPC's work. And again, the "American Presbyterian" party took up the task of overruling the Committee on Foreign Missions. The same theological problems were debated afresh, but now they were clothed in the rhetoric of missions and the nature of the call to the ministry. Commissioners on both sides of the debate presented vigorous speeches, but the assembly could not reach a decision about whether to send Hamilton. What finally broke the deadlock was the reelection of Murray to the Committee on Foreign Missions by the margin of a single vote. At this point the coalition supporting Clark began to disintegrate. Hamilton withdrew as a missionary and others resigned from membership on various committees. This began a gradual withdrawal of significant ministers (e.g. Clark, Strong, and Hamilton) and congregations from the OPC. Clark, who in 1945 had become professor of philosophy at Butler University, would eventually join the United Presbyterian Church of North America.

Still, the great theological issues raised in the Clark controversy had not been resolved. To that end the General Assembly of 1947 appointed yet a third committee, again including Murray and Stonehouse. This body presented to the assembly the following year a ninety-six page document which was printed in the Minutes and contained a majority report and four minority reports. In the end, the doctrinal position of the faculty of Westminster Seminary prevailed, especially because of the strength of the majority report.

Several factors were at work in this controversy. One important difference between Clark and the faculty at Westminster, especially Cornelius Van Til, concerned divergent apologetical methods. Clark came from a tradition of Protestant apologetics that stressed the reasonableness of the Christian religion and the powers of human logic. He advanced the notion that the intellectual powers of fallen men and women still permitted the recognition of truth, even in spiritual matters. Van Til, in contrast, developed an apologetic for Christianity called presuppositionalism. This outlook took seriously the effects of sin upon human reason. Van Til posited a fundamental antithesis between the intellects of believers and unbelievers. In the same way that the fall caused the will to rebel and the emotions to hate God, so sin also incapacitated the mind from seeing reality truly. In effect, Van Til's understanding of the effects of sin upon the intellect taught, contrary to the modern myth of objective science and disinterested observation, that the mind, as well as the will and emotions, was prone to distort reality in the interests of sinful human nature.

But the Clark controversy involved more than different schools of defending the faith. This explains why Murray, not Van Til, emerged as the chief critic of Clark. Indeed, it is significant, contrary to the impression created by referring to this conflict as the "Clark–Van Til Controversy," that Van Til did not write about the affair until 1949, after the crisis had ended. Clark's overestimation of the ability of the mind to see truth accurately apart from the work of the Holy Spirit had important and pernicious theological consequences. Not only did Clark's views imply that regeneration was unnecessary for some true knowledge, but the idea that human knowledge, even that of unbelievers, was the same in some ways to God's knowledge, appeared to contradict the clear teaching of Scripture and the Reformed confessions that an enormous chasm exists between the sovereign Lord of the universe and his finite creation, even those creatures who bear the divine image. Van Til's apologetics, in other words, started with the fundamental Reformed teaching about the fall and the necessity of grace for all human endeavors. What is more, Van Til's teaching underscored the Calvinistic emphasis upon God's sovereignty and glory. God's revelation and activity in removing the blinding effects of sin were at the heart of Van Til's system, not the character and power of the human mind. As Murray wrote in 1946, the issue was not apologetical methods but rather "the place that the transcendent mystery of God's being, perfections, counsel and will should occupy both in our thinking and in our theology." In sum, Clark failed to express unequivocally a God-centered understanding of the Christian religion.

The OPC, therefore, emerged from the Clark controversy with firm convictions about certain biblical truths: that the incomprehensible God, who is always incomprehensible to finite minds, has revealed himself to us so that we know him truly; that while truth is one there is also a qualitative distinction between God's knowledge and ours; that there is also a difference between the knowledge of the believer and the unbeliever because of the enlightening effects of regeneration in the former and the blinding effects of unregenerate human nature in the latter; that God in his wisdom has revealed profound truths which are beyond the capacity of human reason to reconcile, such as divine predestination and man's free agency; and that the free offer of the gospel to all men expresses God's true desire that all men should be saved and come to the knowledge of him.

The irony that emerged during this controversy should not be overlooked. The OPC, because of its careful adherence to the Westminster Standards, has long been criticized as overly rationalistic and intellectual. The Reformed faith, according to its critics, does not properly acknowledge the role of the Holy Spirit or the influence of the will and emotions in saving faith and knowledge of God. The typical caricature of Reformed theology is that salvation is the logical result of accepting certain rational propositions

about God, Jesus, and the Bible. The Clark controversy demonstrates how far from the mark such objections are. For despite the
OPC's high regard for the Westminster Standards and the value of
theological reflection for the church, throughout the Clark controversy came clear affirmations of the primacy of the Holy Spirit,
the fallenness of human reason, and the inability of men and wom-
en to comprehend the mysterious ways of a righteous and holy
God.

The Character of the OPC

As much as the controversy surrounding Clark's ordination
concerned core convictions of the Reformed faith, it also said a
good deal about the OPC. As indicated above, in the background
of these debates was a battle over the denomination's relations to
evangelical churches and parachurch organizations. Clark's most
vociferous supporters wanted the OPC to be a church for all who
opposed modernism. Evangelicals, from this perspective, were welcome in the church as long as they fought liberal theology. Clark's
opponents, however, wanted the church's identity to be explicitly
Reformed. While Reformed theology includes a firm rejection of
modernism, defending and propagating the system of doctrine
taught by the Westminster Standards was at the heart of the
church's mission. By provoking Clark's departure from the church
along with that of his most vocal backers, the controversy deci-
sively shaped the OPC's identity and relationship to other American Protestants.

Interestingly enough, almost at the same time that the ordination of Clark sparked lively debates in the OPC, the denomination
was forced to consider its connections to a new presence in American Protestantism. In 1942 the National Association of Evangelicals (NAE) was founded to organize and represent the interests of
conservative Protestants who were at odds with the vision of
mainline Protestantism as represented by the liberal agency, the
Federal Council of Churches (now the National Council of
Churches). In a number of national affairs, military chaplaincy,
access to radio, and documents for foreign missions, conservative
Protestants had no means other than the Federal Council for ad-
dressing the federal government. In addition, the NAE sponsored

a number of projects designed to promote a revival of Christianity in the United States and restore the nation to its religious and moral heritage. Though its leaders recognized that mainline churches were tainted by modernism, the NAE did not bar ministers and churches which were still members of a liberal denomination. After all, the conservatives who remained in the mainline Presbyterian Church also needed many of the services that the NAE would provide. The NAE's first president was the nationally recognized pastor of Boston's Park Street Church, Harold John Ockenga, a graduate of Westminster Seminary, an ally of Machen for a time in the 1930s and, consequently, well-known in the OPC.

The OPC was invited but refused in 1943 to join the NAE. A major obstacle was the NAE's inconsistent position on modernism. How could a body that was opposed to liberalism allow its president, Ockenga, to retain his membership in a modernist denomination, the United Congregational Churches of Christ? By not opposing modernism in a consistent way, the NAE's voice would always be compromised. Even more objectionable was the constituency of the new organization, which was composed of different Protestant theological traditions from Pentecostals to Presbyterians. Such a divergent assortment of doctrinal positions would weaken the NAE, forcing it to find a least-common-denominator theology for its activities. Finally, the OPC criticized the NAE's plans to conduct evangelism and missions. These activities were properly a part of the visible church's tasks and were not to be undertaken by a parachurch organization which had no system of oversight by or accountability to church officers.

At its Twelfth General Assembly in 1945 the OPC forged its policies on ecumenicity. In spite of doctrinal and governmental errors in non-Reformed churches, "churches other than Reformed communions" should be recognized as "manifestations of Christ's body." But because of these impurities, the OPC could not unite with denominations outside the Reformed faith. For this reason the church affiliated in 1948 with the Reformed Ecumenical Synod (RES). This fellowship had been founded in 1946 to maintain and defend the Reformed faith throughout the world and was comprised of Reformed and Presbyterian churches from Northern Europe, South Africa, Indonesia, and America. The only churches to join the RES from the United States were the OPC, the Christian Reformed Church, and the Free Magyar Reformed Church in America. By seeking fellowship in an international community that was Reformed rather than merely conservative, the OPC stood apart from the evangelicals sponsoring the NAE whose theology was broadly conservative but whose purposes were informed more by the religious situation in America than by concern for theological consistency and a high view of the visible church.

It is hard to miss the concurrence of the Clark controversy and the OPC's decisions about ecumenical relations. At the time the Clark controversy started, in 1943, the OPC was considering the NAE's invitation. And at the time the OPC joined the RES, in 1948, the Clark controversy was ending. This timing was not coincidental.

Clark and his supporters wanted the OPC to join forces with other conservatives in the United States. The basis for this union was not the explicitly Reformed views of the Westminster faculty but rather the broad mission of opposing modernism and banding together for effective outreach. In 1943 Clark went so far as to invite all foes of liberalism to join the OPC. Ministers in the OPC who sided with Clark also hoped the church would become more evangelical than Reformed. Floyd Hamilton, for instance, said that instead of squabbling over extra-confessional points like the incomprehensibility of God, the OPC should be "fighting Modernism and unbelief in the world at large." Despite desires to impact the world, Clark and Hamilton were suspicious of the non-American leadership provided by the Westminster faculty such as the Scotsman, Murray, and the Dutchmen, Van Til, Stonehouse, and Kuiper. Clark himself spoke of his desire to preserve "the American tradition in Presbyterianism," and Hamilton accused Westminster's faculty of leading the church into Reformed traditions from "other lands." Most disconcerting to Clark and his defenders was the OPC's diminished influence within the emerging evangelical movement. Instead of leading conservatives, Clark complained, the OPC had assumed the position of "an isolationist porcupine." Hamilton concurred. He declared that the denomination had come to a fork in the road; it could either be a "small, circumscribed, obscure group," or "a thriving, vigorous, militant,

Bible-believing denomination," playing "a definite part in arousing" America to "its deadly peril."

Despite these criticisms of the OPC, the church, by remaining outside the new evangelical movement and by joining an international association of Reformed churches, rejected Clark's vision for the denomination. The OPC was to be a distinctly Reformed denomination as defined by the Westminster Standards, not "evangelical" or "conservative" as defined by the new evangelical movement. Clark's departure from the OPC, and that of several of his supporters, was indicative of the denomination's stand. To be sure, the church would oppose modernism but it would not stop there. Positively, it would defend and propagate Reformed theology and adhere to Presbyterian church government as its faithful witness to God's Word. Leaders of the OPC knew that its Reformed identity would not generate large numbers or huge buildings. According to Paul Woolley, the church could either have "many members and much money and read about itself in the newspapers" or it could promote "a growing revival of the preaching, teaching and application of the biblical and Reformed faith." But it could not have both. In its deliberations during the Clark controversy, the OPC made clear that faithfulness was more important than influence.

Those who left the OPC with Clark were saddened by the church's vision. They believed that the church had been founded to oppose "soul-destroying Modernism" and was now moving away from its original vision. But as we have already seen, the forming of the OPC involved far more than fundamentalist opposition to modernism. Machen was dedicated to maintaining and preserving a Reformed testimony. The 1937 split of the OPC indicated that the church was also committed to Presbyterian faith and practice, not for tradition's sake, but to be true to God's revealed Word. Far from repudiating its origins, the OPC, in the debate over Clark's position and in its deliberations about cooperation with evangelicals, was actually being faithful to the convictions that brought it into existence. To be sure, the OPC's Reformed identity has meant that it has been marginal to what many regard as important and powerful organizations and associations in American church life and culture. But the Bible teaches that God does not use the magnificent and mighty to achieve his ends. Rather, as the apostle

Paul wrote, God uses "jars of clay to show that this all-surpassing power" is from him only. As such, the OPC is always prone to failure and error. The weakness of human efforts and the sufficiency of God's grace also mean that the church has a precious message and a unique task to testify to the wonderful truths of the Reformed faith.

8
The Peniel Dispute

ONE OF THE HALLMARKS of the OPC has been its effort to preserve and perpetuate Reformed piety. The church has been content not merely with defending and maintaining Calvinism as a theological system, but has also been concerned to serve and worship God, both on the Lord's Day and throughout the week, in a way that flows from the great doctrinal truths expressed in the Westminster Confession of Faith and Catechisms. A characteristic expression of the OPC's understanding of Reformed piety was found in the charter for Westminster Seminary: "The Christian life is the fruit of Christian doctrine, not its root, and Christian experience must be tested by the Bible, not the Bible by Christian experience."

The Presbyterian and Reformed approach to the Christian life has throughout the church's history in the United States been opposed and misunderstood by non-Calvinistic evangelicals. In fact, the history of modern evangelicalism can be written as a struggle to circumvent Reformed teachings about Christian experience in order to find what is thought to be a more satisfying and vital awareness of God and his mercy. To be sure, pietism and mysticism were present since the early church. But especially over the past 250 years, American evangelical longings for direct, immediate experience of God's presence and for sure and certain evidence of grace have thrived at the expense of Reformed teachings about the centrality of God's Word and the sufficiency of the means of grace. For instance, church historian Richard F. Lovelace has criticized churches like the OPC for putting correct theology above religious experience. He writes that "doctrinal fidelity has been given such primacy over spiritual reality that those with the wrong system or the wrong theory of inspiration have been read out of the kingdom as worshipers of a false and unbiblical Christ."

While Orthodox Presbyterians may want to phrase that statement differently, the truth remains that the OPC has persistently swum upstream against the flood of popular evangelical ideas which put experience and conduct above doctrine. The church has been sharply critical of the charismatic movement's teachings which over the last forty years have had broad appeal to believers searching for an intense and supernatural awareness of God's power. The OPC, adhering to the Reformed tradition, has insisted, as the Westminster Confession of Faith puts it, that the Bible is the "supreme judge" of all matters of faith, that with the formation of the canon of Scripture the operation of the Holy Spirit is always tied directly to God's revealed Word, and that the "whole counsel of God" is set down in Scripture alone. Because the Reformed doctrine of the Word of God teaches that the work of the Holy Spirit does not occur apart from Scripture, it also directs the believer to look for signs of God's power not in private illuminations or mystical experience but in meditation upon and through interaction with the Scriptures.

The OPC, because of its Reformed convictions, has also been critical of evangelical teachings which minimize the individual believer's struggle with sin. Evangelicals under the influence of Arminian ideas about human depravity and grace have gained broad appeal by offering a variety of how-to techniques for living a good and moral life, and by suggesting that the avoidance of specific sins is proof of salvation. Again, Reformed teaching takes a dim view of such optimistic assessments of the Christian walk. On the one hand, the Westminster Confession states that believers' sanctification will be "imperfect in this life"; our struggle with sin will never be finished this side of glory and, therefore, will never be easy. For this reason the Reformed have conceived of sanctification in terms of warfare. Through the Holy Spirit we do battle with the flesh, or our sinful nature. On the other hand, while admitting that sanctification is a battle, the Reformed tradition has also insisted that the good works done by believers are never entirely good. Even though good works do confirm and assure us of our faith, they are nevertheless, according to the Westminster Confession, "defiled and mixed with so much weakness and imperfection that they cannot endure the severity of God's judgment" because of our lingering corruption. These convictions have nurtured an ethos within the OPC which is suspicious of the myriad of "become-good-soon" schemes that are so prevalent on the airwaves and in the popular religious press.

Thus the OPC's understanding of the Christian life, in both its experiential and ethical dimensions, has made its relationship with mainstream evangelicalism lukewarm and at times strained. Evidence of tensions between the Reformed tradition and American evangelicalism, as we saw in the last chapter, surfaced early in the OPC's history during the Clark case. And while the church emerged from that controversy with a clearer sense of its Reformed identity, by no means was there a uniform understanding of the OPC's doctrine and worship. Instead, another controversy, the Peniel dispute, would follow right on the heels of the Clark case and would also be significant for establishing the Reformed character of the church and for inculcating within the OPC a greater appreciation for the edifying doctrines of the Reformed faith. Indeed, to understand conflicts like the Clark case and the Peniel dispute is to appreciate the denomination's reluctance to enter into fraternal relations with other churches and to grasp its doubts about the wisdom and benefits of parachurch organizations.

The debates over the teachings of the Peniel Bible Conference began in 1948 just as the Clark debates ended, and they would last for two decades. But the origins of Peniel itself go back even before the founding of the OPC. In 1930, individuals from several modernist churches in Schenectady, New York, formed a Bible study. Two teachers from the nearby Albany Bible Institute, Susan Beers and Rhoda Armstrong, assisted in the teaching. Eventually the group met for summer retreats at Lake Luzerne, and organized under the name Peniel Bible Conference. Through the years the teachings at Peniel conferences took on distinct characteristics which some observers called "novel and strange." These distinctives, as we shall see, focused on the process of a believer's sanctification and the guidance of the Holy Spirit.

As the conference grew in size and influence, its leadership branched out to include members of several denominations, including ministers from the OPC. And in 1938, several members of the Bible conference would help in forming Calvary OPC in

Schenectady. Early discussions of Peniel in the OPC, therefore, took place in the Presbytery of New York and New England. In 1952, however, discussions would shift to the Presbytery of Philadelphia when a licentiate named G. Travers Sloyer, who was associated with the Peniel movement, transferred to that presbytery. Since 1950, Sloyer had been supplying the pulpit of Redeemer Church in Philadelphia. In 1952 the Presbytery of Philadelphia voted (13 to 4) to revoke Sloyer's license on grounds that his views on guidance and sanctification were "equivalent to new revelations of the Spirit," a violation of the Westminster Confession (1.6). Sloyer appealed to the general assembly, which ordered his license restored while presbytery reexamined the case. (During this time Sloyer had, contrary to the desires of presbytery, continued to fill the pulpit of Redeemer.) The next year presbytery revoked his license a second time, again citing conflicts with the Westminster Confession. Sloyer's supporters countered that his views on guidance were entirely in harmony with the Scriptures and the confession. They conceded that Sloyer had expressed himself in unguarded ways but claimed that he provided no evidence of holding erroneous views.

By the end of the year Sloyer would be reinstated again, and in July of 1954, he was ordained and installed at Redeemer Church. The controversy did not end at this point, however. It erupted again in August of 1957, when thirteen members of Redeemer Church complained that the session had been delinquent "in its failure to protect the members of the congregation from false doctrines of guidance and sanctification." In their statements the complainants referred to deep discord which had been the result of an attitude of "spiritual exclusiveness" displayed by Peniel supporters. The "cancerous sectarianism" of Peniel had motivated many of the complainants to go so far as to remove their children from Sunday school.

When the complaint was denied by the session an appeal was sent to presbytery. Later in the fall of 1957, the Presbytery of Philadelphia declined to find the session "delinquent" but directed it to engage in "active resistance to these practices." When Sloyer and the session refused to accept this directive, the presbytery voted to dissolve the pastoral relationship between Sloyer and Redeemer Church. Sloyer eventually resigned from the presbytery and, with twenty members of the congregation, withdrew from the OPC. To the very end Sloyer insisted that he had no basic disagreement with the church's confessional standards. In his letter of resignation he charged his opponents with "the disposition to destroy anything or anyone associated or sympathetic with the Peniel Bible Conference." Eventually Sloyer would join the Reformed Church in America.

His departure did not bring an end to the Peniel dispute. In fact, the controversial teachings of Peniel would continue to draw the attention of several general assemblies. In 1961, the Twenty-Eighth Assembly eventually ruled that the Peniel teachings represented "a deviation from the doctrine set forth in the Word of God and our subordinate standards." OP ministers who were members of Peniel were further instructed to "disavow such erroneous views." The next year the assembly followed up this decision by appointing a committee to study the matter of guidance. This committee ultimately produced three reports, the final one being submitted in 1969. Six years earlier, the small remnant of the Redeemer Church had disbanded.

Sanctification and Guidance

Peniel must be understood against the backdrop of larger developments in American evangelicalism. When Machen articulated that Christianity was "a way of life founded upon a doctrine," he was primarily championing the primacy of doctrine over against the triumph of experience in religious modernism. But similar thinking was taking root in evangelical circles. Twentieth-century evangelicalism has increasingly focused on the self. David Wells locates the sources of this fascination with experience in the Second Great Awakening of the nineteenth century, where a concern for soul-winning eclipsed a Calvinistic passion for truth and the glory of God. "Evangelicals, no less than liberals before them whom they berated," Wells writes, "have abandoned doctrine in favor of life." They have tended to reduce piety to technique and make the exercise of specific disciplines (such as quiet time) the key to spiritual growth.

The OPC saw in Peniel teachings just these sorts of subjective approaches to the life of the Christian believer. Peniel thrived upon a series of steps which would assist believers in the process of sanctification, such as "meeting the cross" and "denying Satan." The OPC (contrary to Peniel countercharges) never challenged the role of the believer in appropriating the benefits of salvation. Yet it charged that, according to Peniel teaching, these steps *automatically* produced the intended results, thus displaying a mechanical and perfectionistic understanding of sanctification which oversimplified the complexity of the wrestling with indwelling sin to which Scripture calls all Christians. Further, the OPC claimed that Peniel teaching formalized "the relation of the believer to the Holy Spirit, as if the work of the Spirit were dependent on the will of man."

From the perspective of the OPC, Peniel also asserted a distinct way in which the believer could enjoy communion with the Holy Spirit, and this aspect of the controversy moved debate toward the doctrine of guidance. The assembly stated that the sufficiency of Scripture had to be guarded in any affirmations about the guidance of the Holy Spirit: the Bible was, according to the confession, "the only infallible rule of practice." Defenders of Peniel contended that they taught no new revelations of the Spirit. However, by asserting that the Holy Spirit provides to believers some direct feelings or impressions, or convictions, Peniel was in effect teaching that the Holy Spirit gives special revelation. The Spirit's work, in other words according to Peniel, is not mediated to us through those means which God has ordained for the believer's guidance. In essence, Peniel teaching abstracted or divided the work of the Holy Spirit from the infallible and sufficient rule of the Bible.

In a paper on guidance, John Murray acknowledged that believers, as subjects of the Spirit's work, do have "feelings, impressions, convictions, urges, inhibitions, impulses, burdens, [and] resolutions." But these states of consciousness themselves are not the "direct intimation to us of the Holy Spirit's will." To say so is to commit oneself necessarily to the notion of special revelation. Murray wrote, "The only way whereby we can avoid this error is to maintain that the direction and guidance of the Holy Spirit is through the means which he has provided and that his work is to enable us rightly to interpret and apply the Scriptures in the various situations of life and to enable us to interpret all the factors which enter into each situation in the light of Scripture."

Peniel advocates responded by accusing Murray of limiting and restricting the ministry of the Holy Spirit. Sloyer wrote that Murray's position "raises the sovereignty of that which is written above the sovereignty of the Writer, and fails even to allow the Holy Spirit the right to make that which is covered by the general principles of Scripture specifically applicable to concrete situations." Furthermore, he argued that Murray made the believer's deductions from the Bible, rather than the illuminating work of the Holy Spirit, the final authority in the Christian life. Still, the OPC stuck by Murray. Its leaders believed that Peniel taught views about deduction from the Bible and the illumination of the Holy Spirit in a way that was contrary to Scripture. According to Reformed teaching, the work of the Spirit and the Word of God are inseparable. Only through illumination by the Spirit working with the Word may believers deduce truth from God's Word.

Peniel and the Church

The Peniel debates were complicated by the parachurch status of the Peniel Bible Conference. Peniel was from the start an interdenominational organization whose leaders believed they could best carry out their work by remaining free from ecclesiastical control. While the general assembly did not question the loyalty of OP ministers who were connected with Peniel, it did raise the question "whether more or less unconsciously the commitment to Peniel may not involve them in positions and practices which, in effect, do now or in the long run will weaken their proper commitment to the church."

To be sure, many of the teachings of Peniel were modified and, to an extent, clarified as the debate went on. By their own admission, the leaders of Peniel had grown self-consciously Reformed since the founding of the Bible conference, a process that corrected many erroneous views. And the gradual development of Peniel's theology helps to explain somewhat the charges and denials of Arminianism and perfectionism that were exchanged throughout the debates. Some of the more sensational charges arose from sloppy formulations by lay teachers, and were denied by the Peniel ordained leaders. In fact, many observers felt that each party talked past each other, and defenders of Peniel claimed that the strengths of the work were lost in the focus on the sensational aspects of the movement.

In its response to the Twenty-Seventh General Assembly in 1960, the Peniel Bible Conference reminded the assembly that it was "an independent organization incorporated under the laws of the State of New York" and was "not officially answerable to any other group for its doctrines and practices" nor was it "constitutionally bound by any standards other than the Word of God." An eight-member "Prayer Council" had oversight of Peniel's spiritual affairs. Critics argued that the conference's structure would divide the loyalties of OP ministers who were also members of the Prayer Council, and that Peniel promoted, in the case of the Redeemer congregation, what some labeled as an elitist "church within a church."

While not bound by the Westminster Standards or OP church order, leaders of Peniel insisted that the conference was Reformed. "Let the Orthodox Presbyterian Church understand that Peniel has come to rejoice in the Reformed faith as Christendom's most faithful formulation of Scriptural doctrine." But because of its parachurch status, the movement was free to embrace the Reformed faith selectively. So, for instance, figures within the Peniel Conference asserted that there were distortions in the development of the Reformed tradition. Specifically, some noted the failure to develop the doctrine of sanctification, accusing the Reformed faith of extinguishing the "flame of personal holiness." The Reformed "dull-hearted complacency," Peniel defenders added, needed the healthy corrective provided by the holiness movement and the Methodist tradition. Thus, inconsistency and vagueness plagued Peniel's commitment to the Reformed faith. And OPC critics rightly lamented the "serious lack of clarity and precision" in the theological formulations of the Peniel movement.

For years Peniel leadership urged the OPC to work out these theological difficulties through a joint study committee. The OPC's refusal was judged an "action unworthy of Christian brethren" which "bespeaks little zeal for truth or justice." Yet the church was justifiably reluctant to work with a parachurch organization not subject to ecclesiastical discipline. The church always insisted that its interests in Peniel were limited to ministerial members of the OPC who taught Peniel distinctives and to the peace and purity of OP congregations under Peniel's influence.

The Kress Case: Peniel Revisited

Travers Sloyer died in March of 1976 at the age of fifty-seven, a premature death provoked, friends claimed, by his struggle with the OPC. Ironically, in the next month the church would be forced to reexamine the doctrine of the sufficiency of Scripture which had been at the heart of the Peniel dispute. This issue resurfaced when the Presbytery of Ohio sat as a trial judicatory to consider four charges of error against one of its members, Arnold S. Kress, an OP foreign missionary who grew up in the Peniel movement. Three of the charges focused on Kress's views about the gifts of tongues and prophecy in the church. While serving in Japan, Kress had several "tongues speaking" experiences. The Committee on Foreign Missions brought him back on special furlough to discuss the matter with him. Kress held mildly charismatic views and was careful to distance himself from popular charismatic views, such as the idea of "second blessing." While he did believe that the gifts of tongues and prophecy may be found in the church today, he denied that new infallible revelation accompanied a tongues-speaking experience.

Kress willingly submitted to the strenuous judicial process, recognizing the need for a judicial trial in order for the church to address the issues. After hearing the case, the Presbytery of Ohio found him guilty on one of the three tongues-related charges; it determined that his claim that the gifts of prophecy and tongues may continue in the church was "contrary to the Word of God." Contrary to the way that it was widely reported, the presbytery delivered a verdict of "error," not of "heresy." The presbytery also found Kress guilty of the fourth charge of asserting that the church ought not to exclude ministerial members who "hold serious doctrinal errors such as Arminianism or the denial of infant baptism."

Kress appealed to the general assembly that met the next month, marking the first judicial case to come before the assembly in the forty-year history of the OPC. After more than a day of debate, the assembly voted 72 to 39 to deny Kress's appeal on the tongues-related charge. The assembly also overwhelmingly sustained the presbytery on the other charge. It then passed a resolution affirming the value of Kress's gifts to the church and urging his submission to its decision. Kress eventually left the OPC to join the Christian Reformed Church.

In sustaining the Presbytery of Ohio in its judgment, the assembly affirmed the cessationist view of the gifts of tongues and prophecy, an increasingly unpopular position even among conservative Presbyterians. To put the matter briefly, cessationists teach that tongues and prophecy were designed for imparting revelation to the apostolic church. These gifts therefore ceased with the close of the apostolic office and the completion of the New Testament canon.

Like Peniel's teaching, Kress's views had implications for the doctrine of the Christian life as well. The assembly saw problems in Kress that it had also seen in Peniel. The experience of tongues was irreconcilable with the church's understanding of the sufficiency of Scripture. As Murray noted in the earlier debate, the illuminating work of the Holy Spirit is always with and through God's revelation in the Bible. The practice of tongues-speaking, Kress's denials to the contrary notwithstanding, inevitably entails new guidance from the Holy Spirit. Interpreted tongues are, as Richard B. Gaffin, Jr., expressed it in his book *Perspectives on Pentecost*, "functionally equivalent to prophecy," and a claim to prophecy in this age compromises the authority of the Scriptures as the church's only rule for faith and practice.

Conclusion

The distinctive teachings of the Peniel Bible Conference began as a reaction against a perceived sterility in the Christian life. As the debate developed within the church, Peniel advocates believed that such sterility characterized the OPC. In his letter of resignation to the Presbytery of Philadelphia, Sloyer charged that the church was "long on theory, heavy on intellect, and short on warmth, Christian love and evangelistic zeal."

But Sloyer's critics were rightly sensitive to this charge and denied its substance. As Ned Stonehouse put it, "there is assuredly great need among us to lay stress upon true experience and life. Churches or groups concerned for orthodoxy, as history has often taught, may succumb to dead orthodoxy. . . . In rejecting certain conceptions and procedures as not being biblical let us not lose sight of the goal of genuine holiness and spirituality towards which we must press with great earnestness and faithfulness." The issue of the relation between doctrine and experience went back to the controversies that led to the founding of the OPC. Liberal Protestants and some evangelicals judged doctrine by the criteria of experience. But for Machen and the OPC, as the Peniel dispute makes clear, experience is always to be judged by correct doctrine, by the teaching of God's Word. True and genuine experience flows from true and biblical teaching. The problem the OPC and other Reformed believers have witnessed is that Calvinistic piety is not flashy or obvious. Rather, the work of the Spirit and the preaching of the Word make their mark in incremental and often hidden ways. In sum, because Reformed believers do not do all of the things that other Christians believe to be "spiritual" does not mean that the Reformed faith hinders a warm and vital relationship with God. Just as the Reformed rejected many of the practices of Roman Catholic spirituality, so they have also been critical of the excesses of evangelicalism.

It also needs to be said that the OPC evaluated Peniel in the context of its earlier struggles, namely, the battles that led to the formation of the OPC and those which prompted the Clark controversy. For Peniel supporters, this perspective prevented the church from focusing adequately on the real issues. Don Mostrom accused Murray in 1961: "I have watched with growing apprehension the appearance of coldness, withdrawal, stubborn insistence on thinking evil of us, unwillingness to know us and what we actually believe, angry oratory, and inflexibility on your part." If the OPC engaged in angry oratory, it was often returned in kind. One Peniel sympathizer suggested, in a letter to the *Presbyterian Guardian*, that an ulterior motive of Peniel's critics was to "have the OPC remain small." In a sense, this accusation had a point. The OPC's concerns about spirituality and the Christian life were out of step with broader developments in the evangelical world, and the church correctly saw, as it did in the Clark case, that if it was to retain its Reformed identity it could not worry about numbers or larger spheres of influence.

In the end, the church insisted that genuine holiness cannot be obtained apart from Scripture, the only infallible rule for faith and obedience. The Peniel controversy and the related Kress case testify to the OPC's fundamental commitment, of a piece with the Reformed faith, to the sufficiency of Scripture. It is significant that these cases came on the heels of the Clark debate. Just after the church faced the accusations of irrationalism (in the Clark case), Peniel prompted accusations that it was drifting toward "cold dead rationalism" (in Sloyer's words). In truth, the church was seeking to defend the sufficiency of Scripture against both rational and mystical impulses that would usurp biblical authority. Against both threats the church determined to remain biblically Reformed.

The Peniel controversy also says something about the way the OPC resolves theological disputes. Altogether, the debate in its various forms lasted over two decades, taxing the energies of four churches, two presbyteries, and several general assemblies. Although the Peniel movement had disrupted other churches and Christian institutions over these years, in no other setting had the conflict been as protracted. As the *Presbyterian Guardian* commented, "It seems that the OPC has almost leaned over backwards to avoid any semblance of hasty or careless judgment before taking final action." What the *Guardian* perceived as patience, others saw as unbearable delays, and there have been subsequent suggestions for how the church should speed up the judicial process.

Unlike sister denominations such as the Presbyterian Church in America, the OPC has deliberately avoided the establishment of judicial commissions to adjudicate theological disputes speedily. Similarly, at the general assembly there is an unspoken antipathy toward taking parliamentary steps to "close debate" on matters on the floor. Perhaps the church is haunted by memories of Machen and the bureaucratic tyranny that he experienced during his trial.

By executing its task through the deliberate procedures of Presbyterian polity, the OPC seems out of step with a culture that thrives upon speed and immediacy. Without a doubt, the OPC's unattractive features contribute to the church's bellicose image: it has been called, as noted earlier, the "little church with the big mouth." Yet its deliberateness allows the OPC to reflect more thoroughly in theological debate. The experience of the church seems to confirm the point that Dr. Machen made so eloquently: if Christianity is "a way of life founded upon doctrine," then no amount of time debating that doctrine can be considered wasted.

9

The OPC and Ecumenical Relations

WHEN THE COMMISSIONERS to the Forty-Second General Assembly of the OPC convened on May 29, 1975, there was no doubt about the main item on their agenda. Meeting concurrently with the general synod of the Reformed Presbyterian Church, Evangelical Synod, at Geneva College in Beaver Falls, Pennsylvania, the assembly was prepared to debate and vote on a Plan of Union that would unite the two churches.

The RPCES itself was the product of a 1965 merger of two denominations, the Reformed Presbyterian Church (General Synod) and the Evangelical Presbyterian Church. The former included Gordon Clark and other ministers who left the OPC in the 1940s (Clark himself having left the United Presbyterian Church of North America after its merger with the PCUSA in 1958). The Evangelical Presbyterian Church was the product of a division in the Bible Presbyterian Church in the 1950s, and so included many who had left the OPC in the split of 1937. Among the RPCES leaders was Francis Schaeffer, who had studied with Machen and Van Til and who, after leaving the OPC, became a colleague of Carl McIntire.

The 1975 Plan of Union, therefore, was an attempt to heal the wounds of the past decades. In the words of the plan's preamble, "We do not claim to have achieved unanimity of opinion on all the issues that led to that division, but in effecting this union we do confess that the unity of Christ's church should not have been broken as it was in 1937. . . ." The document went on to express

135

regret that neither party had pursued reconciliation and the hope of "the joy of restored fellowship" that would result from reunion.

The agenda for the general assembly informed commissioners of the carefully orchestrated way in which the vote would take place. On Tuesday evening, the two bodies would convene in the Geneva College field house for a joint worship service where they would hear Schaeffer preach. Then at the twilight of his ministry as director of the L'Abri Fellowship of Switzerland, Schaeffer exhorted the combined assemblies to put to rest the animosities of the past and "fix the chasm in the right place" by uniting and fighting common enemies, such as secularism and theological liberalism.

On the next day, after a full day of debate, each assembly was to vote at 4:15 p.m. on the question "Shall the Orthodox Presbyterian Church and the Reformed Presbyterian Church, Evangelical Synod be united to form the *Reformed Presbyterian Church* on the basis of the Plan of Union submitted herein?" The OPC met in a cramped lecture hall in the basement of the Geneva College science building. The RPCES met in the chapel of Old Main, barely fifty yards away. After the simultaneous vote, the stated clerks of each denomination were to meet halfway, and exchange the results.

Following spirited debate, the OPC commissioners voted 95 to 42 in favor of union, securing by a margin of four votes the necessary two-thirds majority. No one was expecting the shock that soon followed. Stated clerk Richard Barker returned to announce to the commissioners that only fifty-seven percent of the RPCES delegates approved the merger, falling far short of a two-thirds majority. For many in the OPC, this vote was a devastating blow; for others, a narrowly averted mistake.

Joining and Receiving

This would not be the only time that the OPC almost voted itself out of existence. In 1981, the general assemblies of the OPC, the RPCES, and the eight-year-old Presbyterian Church in America all approved a plan of "joining and receiving." By this procedure the OPC and the RPCES would both join and be received by the larger PCA, a process designed to simplify the complications of lengthy merger negotiations. Having secured the assent of all three assemblies, the proposal was sent to each denomination's presbyteries, where it had to secure three-fourths majorities. The PCA presbyteries approved a joining and receiving with the RPCES, but they narrowly rejected the proposal with the OPC. Needing a 19 to 6 favorable vote, the proposal received a 17 to 8 majority (one presbytery voted 20 to 20, with the tie considered a "no").

The PCA soon re-extended an invitation, and so the OPC debated "joining and receiving" again, this time at its 1986 Assembly. After sixty-seven speeches, the assembly voted 78 for and 68 against "joining and receiving," considerably short of a three-fourths majority. The next day a protest signed by thirty-eight commissioners was circulated which claimed that the decision was "a serious setback to our hopes for a united, vital, biblical and nationwide Presbyterian church" and that the vote communicated an "attitude of superiority" on the part of the OPC. Several of the commissioners would return to their churches frustrated with the OPC's failures of the past decade to join with other conservative Presbyterian denominations. Some of these pastors and elders persuaded their congregations to withdraw from the OPC and "voluntarily realign" with the PCA.

There are perhaps as many explanations for these actions as there were different reasons for the commissioners' votes. Advocates of the merger efforts of 1975, 1981, and 1986 argue that the OPC should unite with bodies that hold the same confessional standards. Refusal to do so is backward, inward, and exclusive— not biblical, charitable, and wise. Opponents were not convinced that these sister institutions affirmed the Westminster Standards in acceptable ways. At the heart of this concern was the question of what it means to be "Reformed"; e.g., would a Reformed church tolerate Arminian and charismatic office bearers? The heated debates on the floor of the OP general assembly brought to light questions about the theological identities of the denominations involved in discussions.

On the other hand, the OPC has been left at the altar of church union because its suitors have perceived the church to be theologically narrow. John Mitchell, editor of the *Presbyterian Guardian*, speculated that the 1975 vote may have been the result of RPCES fears that the battles of the 1930s and 1940s would be fought again in a united church. Much to the surprise of the synod, Schaeffer, the day after his impassioned speech for merger, reversed himself and spoke critically of union with the OPC shortly before the vote. If the prospect of merging with a contentious church dissuaded some, it was a feature for which many in the OPC refused to apologize. According to OP minister Robert Graham, "It is clear from anyone who knows the history of the OPC that our denomination is not popular because it has consistently been a Machen-type of contending church. Call it 'theological expertise' if you will; but I say, 'Thank God for it.' The OPC has never shunned doctrinal issues thrown at it."

Ironically, the OPC has been blamed in two ways for failing to merge with other denominations. On the one hand, the church's strict Reformed convictions established a difficult set of criteria for finding suitable partners. And on the other hand, those denominations closest to the OPC regarded those very same Reformed convictions as too exclusive and parochial.

Early Efforts at Ecclesiastical Union

One of the lingering criticisms of the OPC is that Machen and his allies, upon leaving the PCUSA in 1936, did not join another Presbyterian denomination already in existence. This question has been raised recently by John Frame in his book *Evangelical Reunion*. Frame, a former OPC member, claims that the founders of the denomination erred by not joining existing bodies, such as the Christian Reformed Church or the Reformed Presbyterian Church, General Synod. Such a charge, however, reveals a good deal of ignorance about OP history. For as Lawrence Eyres correctly observes, in its early years the OPC was an ecclesiastical orphan. No other church would have it.

The OPC's first serious union conversations were with the Reformed Presbyterian Church, General Synod (as noted above, one of the predecessors to the RPCES). Union talks were commissioned by the Twelfth General Assembly of the OPC in 1945. A committee to explore union reported that while significant differences in doctrine and practice needed to be worked out, "the Orthodox Presbyterian Church has a solemn obligation to seek to

effect the visible manifestation of the unity of the body of Christ.
. . . It is incumbent upon us to explore every avenue which may
lead to union." Talks continued for several years, but ended when
a disappointed committee reported to the 1949 General Assembly
that the RPCGS was "unwilling to give serious attention to the
question of union of the two churches." At that point the special
committee was dissolved.

The church then began extensive merger discussions with the
Christian Reformed Church. Although the CRC sent a telegram
of greetings to the OPC's First General Assembly in 1936, it would
be ten years before the CRC sent a fraternal delegate to the OPC
assembly. In the early years of the OPC's existence, many in the
CRC were suspicious of whether the young church would be willing to take strong stands on such issues as membership in lodges.
Others wondered whether the church would prove faithful in ex-
ercising church discipline.

Gradually, though, the CRC warmed up to the OPC. The
CRC magazine, *The Banner*, praised the young church for having
"engaged in heroic warfare against the forces of liberalism in this
country." It went on to claim that "there is no denomination in
this country which has so many things in common with our own"
than the OPC, and that the two churches were "getting closer together." Especially encouraging to the CRC were the OPC's emphases on catechetical instruction and Christian education.
Another tie between the two denominations was the forceful and
wise leadership provided to the OPC by Cornelius Van Til, Ned
Stonehouse, and R. B. Kuiper, members of Westminster Seminary's faculty who had roots in and strong connections to the
CRC.

In 1956 each church established a committee to deepen their
ecclesiastical relationships, and in the following year both committees passed a joint resolution that read:

> In view of the unity of the body of Christ and in view of the basic
> community that exists between the Christian Reformed Church
> and the Orthodox Presbyterian Church in doctrine, polity, and
> practice, it is an obligation resting upon these two Churches to
> make every endeavor to bring this unity and community to their
> consistent expression in the organic union of the two denomina-
> tions.

No one predicted that the task would be simple. Union talks faced the difficulties of harmonizing different doctrinal standards, since the CRC holds to the "three forms of unity" of the continental Reformation: the Belgic Confession, the Heidelberg Catechism, and the Canons of the Synod of Dort. There were also questions about harmony between CRC and OPC standards of polity and worship.

Up until 1966 progress toward union appeared to be going apace. Both churches had begun to cooperate in home and foreign missions, youth programs, a system of pulpit exchange, and publishing efforts. However, concerns began to arise in the OPC about the CRC, and in 1967, the OPC general assembly gave a mandate to the committee on ecumenical relations which called for an investigation into "trends toward liberalism" in the CRC, especially with regard to biblical infallibility and the doctrine of creation. Some in the OPC felt that the CRC was departing from its creedal commitments, and they drew parallels between developments in the CRC and the history of modernism in the Presbyterian Church. Many in the CRC, however, felt betrayed by what they perceived was a sudden and unwarranted change of direction in the OPC. Union discussions cooled significantly and ended completely in 1972.

Altogether, the OPC has had serious discussion with four different denominations. What is important about all of these episodes is that they betray a commonly held but false impression of the Orthodox Presbyterian Church, namely, that it is an isolated collection of theological precisionists. Those that lodge such charges are unaware of the church's many efforts throughout its history to explore union with other denominations committed to the Reformed faith. Since its founding the OPC has had an ongoing interest in ecumenicity, and its failure to unite with other churches is as much due to the refusal of others as to any stubbornness of its own.

The "Ecumenical Imperative"

The desire to unite with other confessionally similar bodies stems from the "ecumenical imperative" of Scripture. This imperative is not a recent development within the OPC. Since its founding in 1936, the OPC clearly understood that it was not, from its small corner of the Reformed world, the sole possessor of truth and wisdom. On the contrary, it has sought diligently the wisdom of sister denominations. Much of the ecumenical leadership came from the faculty of Westminster Seminary where a number of the members, due to their ecclesiastical backgrounds, were a constant reminder of the witness to the Reformed faith in other parts of the world and in other churches in North America.

For many Christians, the word "ecumenical" connotes the negative image of liberal churches in the World Council of Churches. Ned Stonehouse insisted, however, that it was an important word in the vocabulary of Christian orthodoxy. "The difference between the orthodox and Modernists in their striving for unity," he wrote, "is that the former insist that the unity must not be sought or achieved at the expense of purity in doctrine and life as judged by the standard of the Holy Scripture."

The New Testament speaks often of the need for Christians to manifest visible unity. In his prayer in John 17, Jesus sought a *visible* unity of the church that reflected the perfect unity between him and God the Father. In Ephesians Paul speaks of one body and one faith, a unity of the Spirit in the faith. This unity transcends all cultural diversity, according to Galatians 3:28. While this unity may be thought by some to refer exclusively to the invisible church, a 1945 OPC report entitled "Scriptural Principles of Cooperation with Other Churches" stressed that the "visible church must manifest in particular the unity of the invisible church."

At the same time this report added that "in no case may the Orthodox Presbyterian Church in its cooperation with other churches sacrifice, or even compromise, its distinctiveness." What, then, is the OPC's distinctiveness? It is not merely its Reformed standards but its zeal in adhering to those standards, according to the report. The tension between theological distinctiveness and ecclesiastical union is not easily solved. All contemporary denominations, the OPC included, have arisen out of unique ethnic identities or historical circumstances. These have in turn produced healthy traditions that bind members with a sense of common identity. But can these traditions impede faithfulness to the ecumenical imperative? It is likely that the 1986 vote against union with the PCA was influenced by the celebration, at that same assembly, of the OPC's semi-centennial. The sustained reflection on the church's first fifty years and the reminder of the sacrifices of the first generation probably dissuaded some commissioners from joining a larger and more diverse body. Was this a case, as critics accused, of theological inwardness? Or does tradition give communities a "binding address" in an increasingly fragmented world?

It has been said in jest that the OPC stands for the "Only Pure Church." But the OPC has always recognized that it is not *the* church, not the *only* true church on earth. It believes the Westminster Confession that teaches that all churches—including the OPC—are "more or less pure" and that "the purest churches under heaven are subject both to mixture and error." Sharing the perspective of historic Presbyterianism on the "pluriformity" of the church, the OPC acknowledges that the visible, universal church consists of "all those persons in every nation, together with their children, who make profession of saving faith in the Lord Jesus Christ and promise submission to his commandments" (Form of Government, II.2). Thus conservative Baptist, Lutheran, and Methodist churches are, despite their errors, churches of Jesus Christ.

The OPC's 1945 statement on cooperation insisted that the church "is in sacred duty bound to seek organic union with these churches." Further, "complete unanimity on every detail of doctrine and practice" is not "a prerequisite for union." Yet unity cannot come at the price of the truth. And so, as John Galbraith has written, the OPC has "endeavored to walk the fine line between indiscriminate ecumenism and indiscriminate sectarianism."

In light of the church's ecumenical efforts since its founding, it seems hard to believe that, nearly sixty years later, it is still a small denomination. God has sovereignly chosen to frustrate the desires of many in the church for a larger denomination with more visibility and recognizable influence. But the church should not be discouraged by its size or its limited stature. As John Galbraith wrote in the *New Horizons,*

> This we must do: be humble, be patient, bear with one another, teach one another, learn from one another, grow in grace, work for unity and pray for unity. We have this assurance: when we, by God's grace working in our hearts, do his will, he will bless us, he will bless

his church, he will glorify his own name. And God will see to it in his own way and his own time that *we* and *they* will become *us*.

Ecumenicity and International Calvinism

The 1945 report on cooperation did not reduce the "ecumenical imperative" to efforts aimed at achieving ecclesiastical union. Instead, it urged the church to pursue other sorts of relations with truly Reformed churches in the interest of spreading the Reformed faith. At the 1975 General Assembly, which saw plans for union with the RPCES fail, the OPC took another significant step in expanding its ecumenical efforts. In that year, the OPC helped to form NAPARC, the North American Presbyterian and Reformed Council. Along with the OPC, charter members included the Christian Reformed Church, the Presbyterian Church in America, the Reformed Presbyterian Church, Evangelical Synod, and the Reformed Presbyterian Church of North America. Present membership now includes the Associate Reformed Presbyterian Church and the Korean American Presbyterian Church. All of these churches expressed full commitment to the infallibility of the Bible and to Reformed confessional standards.

NAPARC was founded to "advise, counsel, and cooperate in various matters with one another and hold out before each other the desirability and need for organic union of the churches that are of like faith and practice." The work of the council includes the reaching of a comity agreement for church planting and consultations on Christian education and missions. Recently, NAPARC has discussed members' concerns over doctrinal issues in the Christian Reformed Church.

Extending beyond American borders, the OPC has assumed a role of leadership in international Calvinism. In 1948 the church sent a representative to the inaugural meeting of the International Council of Christian Churches, a conservative alternative to the World Council of Churches. But after a four-year effort to steer the constitution of the ICCC in a Reformed direction failed, the OPC withdrew from participation.

The church established a more fruitful relationship for international ecumenical relations with the founding in 1946 of the Reformed Ecumenical Synod. The OPC sent a representative to the RES's first meeting, and soon thereafter it joined. From that first conference, with delegates from three churches in attendance, the RES grew to include thirty churches in eighteen countries. Its goal was to strengthen member churches and to assist them in maintaining soundness of faith and practice. Unlike the ICCC, it sought to preserve a distinctive Reformed character through shared commitments to Reformed confessions. As Stonehouse enthusiastically described it, the RES "serves to take churches out of their isolation and absorption with their own problems and perspectives and affords an opportunity for a contemplation of the world-wide mission of the church of Jesus Christ."

For these reasons, the OPC joined the RES enthusiastically and sent delegates faithfully to meetings every four years. For most of these years there were opportunities for the OPC to exert international leadership within a body representing a total membership approaching five million. It was the OPC, for example, that initiated RES discussions in the church about apartheid (see chapter twelve).

Conflicts developed in the 1970s, however, regarding the wavering commitment of some of the RES member churches to the Reformed creeds and over the synod's failure to exercise discipline over its membership. For instance, as early as the 1950s the Reformed Churches in the Netherlands (GKN), a member of RES, joined the World Council of Churches. The OPC sought to persuade the synod to regard such membership as incompatible with RES membership, but was unsuccessful. The GKN proceeded into further theological difficulties, and in 1972 the OPC sent a letter to all RES churches, challenging the creedal fidelity of the GKN. Specifically, the OPC expressed concerns over the GKN's ordination of women, its interpretation of early chapters of Genesis, and its doctrine of Scripture. In 1979 the GKN again pushed the limits of fraternal relations in the RES by permitting homosexual relationships in the church. Because of the RES's unwillingness to address these matters, and after nearly a decade of debate, the OPC resigned its RES membership in 1988.

Still committed to strengthening the bonds of international Calvinism, the OPC sent observers to the International Conference of Reformed Churches (a smaller body that was founded in 1982). Here the OPC was warmly received as a church that zealously defended the Reformed faith. Both its longstanding commitment to ecumenicity in the RES and its eventual withdrawal from that organization earned for the OPC the immediate trust of this new body. The ecumenical ties with other denominations, especially in Third World settings, have in turn opened mission doors for the church. Recently the Committee on Foreign Missions sent Brian and Dorothy Wingard to Kenya, through contacts that were originally established by the Committee on Ecumenicity and Interchurch Relations with the Reformed Church of East Africa.

Conclusion

Ironically, it could be argued that the OPC's small size has enhanced its international ecumenicity. Humbled by its cultural marginalization in North America, the church has not had to defend the claims or the status of a large national denomination. Providentially kept from the temptation to glory in size and influence, the OPC has been blessed to work with international denominations as full partners. Presently, international ecumenicity has spread to the point where the sun does not set on the churches with whom the OPC shares ecclesiastical fellowship. But unlike the British empire, the OPC has not pursued a policy of imperialism. It seeks to respect the integrity of the established churches in other lands, which is as much a commitment to the unity of the church as any talk of denominational merger. As Jack Peterson has written, the OPC consists of "separatists but not isolationists." It is fully committed to the vision of establishing and maintaining relations with other churches, no matter what their nationality or size, of "like precious faith."

PART FOUR
THE MINISTRY
OF THE CHURCH

IN THE SPRING OF 1926, J. Gresham Machen made what turned out to be a very controversial decision. At the meeting of his presbytery, a fellow minister submitted a resolution supporting the federal government's policy of making the sale and production of beverage alcohol illegal. Machen voted against the resolution and probably thought little about his voice vote.

But at the 1926 General Assembly this vote turned out to be one of the chief reasons why he was denied promotion to the chair of apologetics at Princeton Seminary. Liberals and conservatives in the Presbyterian Church vigorously supported Prohibition, and anyone who gave the slightest evidence of dissent was assumed to be immoral. When Machen explained his action he said that while he opposed drunkenness, he opposed more the mindset which made the church an agency of law enforcement. By supporting Prohibition as part of its formal activities, he argued, the Presbyterian Church was "in danger of losing sight of its proper function, which is that of bringing to bear upon human souls the sweet and gracious influences of the gospel." Machen added that while the functions of the police and law enforcement were worthwhile pursuits for Christians to support "as individuals," "the duty of the Church in its corporate capacity is of quite a different nature."

Machen's actions flowed from his belief that the church's task was essentially spiritual. It was not an agency of social welfare, a political lobby, or even an institution for promoting worthwhile cultural or educational endeavors. Instead, Machen regarded the church primarily as a message-bearing institution and looked to the risen Christ's words to his disciples—"You shall be my witnesses"—as the founding principle of the church. Christianity, in other words,

> is not a life as distinguished from a doctrine, or a life which has doctrine as its flower and fruit, but—just the other way around—it is life founded upon a doctrine. It is a life produced not merely by exhortation, not merely by personal contacts, but primarily by an ac-

count of something that happened, by a piece of good news, or a gospel.

This conception of Christianity informed Machen's understanding of the ministry, and it continues to lie at the heart of the OPC's teaching about the church as an institution. The church has an essential task, one not shared by any other institution, which is to proclaim the good news about Christ. This is a highly propositional and educational task, for it is rooted in the fact that God ordained the preaching of his Word as the means by which he draws his children to himself. This view of the church also puts a premium upon doctrinal instruction and theological understanding. As Machen rightly saw, and as the Reformed faith has historically maintained, the Bible is from beginning to end theological. To understand the Bible is to understand doctrine. For this reason, the OPC has stressed the importance of theology, not just for the ministers, though it perpetuates the Reformed tradition's pattern of treasuring an educated ministry, but also for all members of the church.

In the chapters that follow on the ministry of the church these themes are developed. The OPC's commitment to theology is evident in its program of Christian education. The distinctive task or nature of the church is developed in the next two chapters. The highest calling of God's people is to worship the Lord, and worship is ultimately the direction to which the church's special work tends. The spiritual character of the church's ministry is also evident in the OPC's handling of social matters. While individual members of the denomination have been properly concerned about many of the political and cultural struggles that vex American society, the church has shied away from taking a corporate stand on issues which lie properly within the spheres of the state or the family. The OPC thus bears the stamp of Machen's vision for the church, an institution whose unique purpose and privilege is to proclaim the good news about Christ and bring souls into sweet communion with the living and true God.

10
A "Full-orbed and Consistent" Christian Education

THE COVENANT THEOLOGY that lies at the center of the Reformed tradition makes education a solemn obligation for God's people. Repeatedly throughout the Old Testament God reminds believers of the chief importance of instruction in the faith. The education of children in the ways of the covenant is an especially prominent theme in Scripture. For instance, in Deuteronomy Moses reminds the Israelites of the awesome responsibility of instructing their children in the truths of God's Word:

> And these words which I command you this day shall be upon your heart; and you shall teach them diligently to your children and shall talk of them when you sit in your house, and when you walk by the way, and when you lie down, and when you rise. And you shall bind them as a sign upon your hand, and they shall be as frontlets between your eyes. And you shall write them on the doorposts of your house and on your gates (Deut 6:6–9).

Psalm 78 reiterates the importance of this duty. Not only were God's people to know the law, but they were also to know and teach to their children the great and miraculous deeds of God's redemption. "We will not hide them from their children," the Psalmist writes, "but tell to the coming generation the glorious deeds of the Lord, and his might, and the wonders which he has wrought." So important is the teaching function of God's people that Scripture often explains the apostasy and infidelity of Israel in terms of their failure to instruct their children in the ways of the covenant (Judges 2:10).

When the OPC was formed in 1936, the church was well aware that the errors of the mainline Presbyterian Church stemmed from a failure to conduct faithfully its educational responsibilities. According to the Christian Education Committee's report at the OPC's Second General Assembly:

> The triumph of unbelief in the old organization was due in no small measure to the prostitution of existing education agencies through compromise with unbelief on the one hand, and to the lack of a full-orbed and consistent system of Christian education on the other.

For this reason, the committee recommended that if the OPC was to be "a truly Reformed church," efforts to construct a comprehensive program of Christian education be started immediately.

The OPC's efforts in the sphere of Christian education have in many ways been remarkable, both for the quality of materials and for the dedication to nurture a deeper understanding of the Christian religion, both in children and adults. And the history of the OPC's educational publications gives further evidence of the denomination's unwavering zeal to propagate and defend the Reformed faith. Yet this story not only reveals the difficulties that confront a small church which strives to undertake a "full-orbed" system of Christian education. It also reflects the obstacles that confront believers who strive to follow the ancient principles of God's covenant while living in a modern society whose values and structures of authority make those very principles unusual, if not implausible.

The Informal and Irregular Curriculum, 1936–1942

When the OPC was founded, the denomination was unified behind the conviction that the mainline Presbyterian Church (PCUSA) had capitulated to the un-Christian theology of modernism. J. Gresham Machen and other OP leaders had made the missions board of the old denomination the focus of their concerns. But they could have easily singled out the mainline denomination's Board of Christian Education, for the signs of liberal theology were equally evident in the literature and programs of that denominational agency.

Machen himself had experienced difficulties with Presbyterian officials responsible for Christian education almost twenty years before the founding of the OPC. In the years just prior to World War I, he wrote *A Rapid Survey of the Literature and History of the New Testament Times*. This book has been reprinted as a general introduction to the New Testament (*The New Testament: An Introduction to Its Literature and History*, Banner of Truth, 1976), but was originally part of the Presbyterian Church's series of graded lessons. This particular course was designed for teenagers in senior high school and came complete with student lesson books and teacher's manual. Machen experienced a number of frustrations with the denominational officers who edited the project. His editors were less concerned with the historical and theological content of the New Testament, seeking instead approaches to the material that would inspire the students to be good citizens. Consequently, well before the outbreak of the fundamentalist controversy in the 1920s, Machen detected in the church's education program the characteristic liberal Protestant understanding of Christianity as a system of ethics and good will.

In 1923, in an effort to streamline and centralize denominational activities, the Presbyterian Church created the Board of Christian Education. It took over all the educational endeavors of the denomination, from Sunday schools to denominational colleges. Soon there followed a curriculum for Sunday school that was designed for the education of church members from childhood to old age. This curriculum borrowed heavily from educational theories of the day, many of them derived from John Dewey's philosophy of pragmatism. The goal of such an education was for individuals to realize their full potential as human beings, though the curriculum dressed this aim up with the phrase, "the fullest possible self-realization in Godlikeness." A related aim of the new curriculum was to develop a Christian character, again borrowing from the popular public school notion of "character education." The liberal tendency of this program of study became especially evident in its treatment of the Bible as "the best religious experience of the race" that provided "effective guidance to present experience."

Had Machen and other conservatives wanted to make an issue of such materials, they undoubtedly could have mustered a fight as feisty as the one which took place over missions. Nonetheless, recognition of the state of Christian education in the mainline church is useful not just to see how deeply liberalism permeated the old denomination but also to understand the peculiar difficulties the OPC faced when, at its founding, its leaders sought materials to use in their congregations. Evangelical publishers had a good deal of material to offer. But for a church dedicated to the Calvinistic theology and Presbyterian polity of the Westminster Standards, there were few places to turn for solidly Reformed curriculum and lessons.

To this end the OPC at its First General Assembly established the Committee on Christian Education, which undertook a number of initiatives to provide for the genuine need in the new denomination. Yet its powers at first were primarily advisory. Budgetary demands for home and foreign missions and the economy of the Great Depression left little money for the personnel, publishing, and distribution costs that a full-fledged Christian education program would require. Consequently, the committee recommended to pastors for use in their churches various evangelical and Reformed educational materials that were already available. It also advised pastors and families to form organizations for the purpose of establishing Christian day schools. And recognizing the need for a learned ministry, the committee asked that congregations support Westminster Seminary with prayers and gifts.

One sees in the committee's initial recommendations the breadth of Christian education as understood by the OPC. Christian education concerns more than merely Sunday school. It also involves the so-called secular education of children as well as the theological training of prospective ministers. For this reason the general assembly regularly recommended pastors and church members to form Christian day school societies with a view toward founding Christian schools. While the OPC has always insisted that education is the responsibility not of the church but of the family—and therefore has refused to establish parochial or church schools in the way that Roman Catholics and Lutherans have—the church has also contended that education in the arts and sciences needs to be conducted in a Christian context. Hence the education of covenant children involves not just religious instruction in the Bible and theology but in the other areas of learning as well. A number of thriving Christian schools exist throughout the United States today because of OP efforts, such as

Philmont Christian Academy in Philadelphia and Trinity Christian School in Pittsburgh.

By the time of the Fifth General Assembly in 1939, the Committee on Christian Education obtained the power to receive and disburse funds for the purpose of promoting its work. The committee's beginnings were truly modest. Receipts for the first year amounted only to approximately $300, while expenditures were roughly $180. Clearly the frugality demanded by the Depression era kept the committee well within its budget.

The work which the committee did was also humble but nonetheless impressive for such a small operation. With no general secretary, the burden of conducting Christian education fell to the committee members themselves. Lawrence Gilmore devised summer Bible school materials and Burton Goddard took over single-handedly the preparation, production, and distribution of lessons for young people. This was in partial response to an overture at the Fourth General Assembly in 1938 which proposed the founding of a young people's group throughout the entire denomination called the Machen League. This overture reflected a clear sense of the need for material for teenagers. This need was also evident in the pages of the *Presbyterian Guardian*, the monthly publication which began before the OPC's founding and which was published independently of the denomination, but which functioned as the denominational magazine. In 1938 the *Guardian* started a young people's page which was regularly supplied by Edward J. Young, professor of Old Testament at Westminster Seminary and chairman of the committee on young people's work. His lessons featured instruction on biblical topics such as the person of Christ and messianic prophecies. Later lessons were written by different pastors and professors at the seminary.

Without denominational officers or administrators who specialized in different features of the church's outreach, work such as that required by Christian education had to be picked up by everybody in the church. The experience of the fundamentalist controversy in the mainline Presbyterian Church had also taught Orthodox Presbyterians to be suspicious of denominational agencies which, it seemed, always created more problems than they were worth. Consequently, ministers and elders alike pitched in with the efforts to provide a system of Christian education for the fledgling denomination. The lack of a well established administrative structure and limited resources gave Christian education in the early years of the OPC an ad hoc quality. A mailing with summer Bible school lessons would arrive here, and a different topic and author for the young people's page in the *Presbyterian Guardian* would appear there. Yet, even in its organizationally underdeveloped state, the work of Christian education continued to grow and to be of a remarkably high quality.

For instance, the Committee on Christian Education early on decided to publish a series of long tracts which were intended for adults and young people. These tracts ranged from apologies for the OPC which explained why the mainline Presbyterian denomination was in error and why the new church had to be formed, to explications of the Bible and the Reformed faith. In the former class belonged John P. Galbraith's *Why the Orthodox Presbyterian Church?* and Murray F. Thompson's *The Auburn Betrayal.* Galbraith's tract expounded the Calvinistic theology for which the OPC stood and delved into the history of the liberal takeover of the mainline church, thus requiring the founding of a new denomination dedicated to God's Word. Thompson's booklet refuted the Auburn Affirmation, a document written in 1923 which became the rallying point for liberals in the Northern Presbyterian Church.

As unusual as these tracts might seem to readers at the end of the twentieth century, they were nevertheless quite essential to the OPC because they staked out the new denomination's identity and reminded church members of the great sacrifices and principles involved in the forming of the OPC. In fact, the Committee on Christian Education hoped that these publications would assist in the recruitment of other pastors and congregations and build alliances with other Reformed denominations. Consequently, the committee decided to have them distributed to seminarians at specific mainline Presbyterian institutions and to pastors in the Christian Reformed Church and the Southern Presbyterian Church. Whatever the merits of this strategy, the early publications of the committee are still valuable for readers today who have questions about the OPC's historical and theological origins.

The other type of long tract sponsored by the Committee on Christian Education featured sound material on Scripture and Reformed theology. One of the first published in this vein was *Is the Bible Right About Jesus?* by J. Gresham Machen. It was a reprint of three lectures he gave during the mid–1920s and contained a solid defense of the historical truthfulness of the New Testament's witness to Jesus Christ. In addition, the committee sponsored *The Covenant of Grace*, by Calvin Knox Cummings, and *The Sovereignty of God*, by John Murray. Each of these tracts developed key themes of Reformed theology and, like the pamphlet by Machen, are still worthy of study and reflection.

As these tracts indicate, the OPC was extremely blessed by a well-educated pastorate, and the work of Westminster Seminary was crucial to this dimension of the denomination's work. Not only did the professors at the seminary regularly write pamphlets for the church, or the young people's page for the *Presbyterian Guardian*, but they often served on church committees and, perhaps most importantly, educated almost all of the OPC's pastors. In this way the early days of the OPC were a throwback to an era before specialization, when professors at seminaries labored for the church as well as in the classroom, and when the levels of education and specialized knowledge did not separate the theological faculty from the clergy, or the clergy from the laity. If the early publications of the Committee on Christian Education are any indication, OPC members, from young people to the Westminster faculty, were all expected to be on the same theological page. In fact, the expectations for uniformity in theological understanding throughout the denomination were especially evident in the minutes of the Eleventh General Assembly, when the Committee on Christian Education not only recommended that congregations support the publication of the *Westminster Theological Journal*, but also that ministers and elders throughout the denomination regularly read the journal "as a means of Christian education." In an age when most theological journals were becoming extinct because of the perception that theological and biblical scholarship had little relevance to people in the pews, the OPC, either courageously or naively, depending on one's perspective, was recommending that its officers study one of the few scholarly publications with genuine Reformed substance.

Early Efforts to Organize, 1943–1955

In 1943 the work of Christian education achieved a measure of stability when the general assembly approved the appointment of Floyd Hamilton as the first full-time general secretary of the Committee on Christian Education, a position which he occupied until 1947. In an effort to have a more systematic program, the committee in 1944 also devised general principles "of Christian education and pedagogy" which would guide the OPC's work. The committee's report, submitted to and approved by the Twelfth General Assembly (1945), said a good deal about the Reformed identity of the OPC and the way in which a Calvinistic church should conceive of its educational functions.

The report starts with the doctrine of the covenant, distinguishes between covenant and non-covenant students within the church, and affirms the priority of educating those included in the covenant community. The committee wrote, "We must place before even the command to evangelize the lost this prior responsibility of bringing up the children of the church in the nurture and admonition of the Lord." The doctrine of the covenant also taught that the church should devise a program with the specific needs of covenant children in mind. Having established the aim of Christian education, the report went on to outline the methods for such instruction of covenant youth.

On the one hand, the demand to conform to Scripture required that education "emphasize the God-given authority and responsibility of the parents and church officers in training the youth." It also included a proper use of and reverence for the Sabbath. "Some methods of teaching perfectly proper on other days ought not to be used on the Lord's Day." On the other hand, the report distanced the OPC from much of the pedagogy and psychology that dominated public school and mainline Protestant Sunday school education. The OPC's materials would be God-centered, not child-centered. "The material of our teaching," the report stipulated, "cannot be subordinated to the child, for, unlike the curriculum of modern pagan education, it is not prepared from sociological considerations for utilitarian goals, but is God's eternal truth." This did not mean, however, that the church should be indifferent to the needs of children. After all, the report reminded,

it was "Christ who set the child in the midst, warning against caus-
ing such to stumble." In fact, no greater concern for the student
could be found than one that stemmed from zeal "for fruit to the
glory of God in the life of each pupil."

Despite such an inspiring and biblically informed rationale for
Christian education, the committee's work continued to operate
on a shoestring. Various individuals, such as Lewis Grotenhuis,
Betty Colburn, Edmund Clowney, Calvin Cummings, and
Dorothy Partington, provided yeoman service in the production of
Bible and Sunday school materials, church bulletins, and short and
long tracts. Often these individuals were underpaid and over-
worked, and their product, while professionally done, rarely ri-
valed in slickness what larger publishing houses could produce.
Nevertheless, like the principles which informed the work of the
committee, the lessons and instructional materials which in 1951
became known as Great Commission Publications were solidly
biblical and Reformed.

The Age of Expansion and Uncertainty,
1955 to the Present

With the appointment of Robley Johnston as general secretary
of the Committee on Christian Education in 1955, the publishing
initiative of OP instructional materials entered a new era, one
much more ambitious and driven by demands outside the denomination. A paragraph from the fifty-year history of the OPC reveals
the change of tone and shift in orientation of the Committee on
Christian Education.

> The early Sunday school materials and young people's materials
> were largely parochial. They involved much labor of love and a sin-
> cere attempt to provide doctrinally sound instruction for the
> churches in the OPC. Their mimeographed format, however, did
> not commend them to congregations outside our denomination.
> Many even of our own congregations seemed to prefer the slick,
> commercially acceptable publications of the major evangelical
> presses to the homegrown product.

Under Johnston's leadership the materials produced by the Committee on Christian Education would remain biblically and theologically sound while becoming more appealing in design. The

committee would also seek to produce material useful for Reformed and evangelical churches beyond the OPC.

The decision to produce materials to be used by other churches was tied to the decision to design a total curriculum for the OPC's congregations. The denomination was, after all, a small one and of modest means. It did not have the resources to subsidize, nor did it represent a large enough market to pay for, a comprehensive curriculum. By 1962 a staff had been assembled to complete a three-year-cycle Sunday school curriculum. The goal was a curriculum "full of Bible content, Reformed in doctrinal outlook, attractively printed, and teachable." Yet the OPC did not have sufficient funds for such an undertaking. Consequently, the general assembly approved in 1962 the Sunday School Publication Loan Fund which was designed to raise sufficient capital to finance the development and publication of a Sunday school curriculum.

The move to serve other Reformed churches through Great Commission Publications encouraged in some the desire for the OPC to become a bigger church with a larger national presence, and for a merger with other conservative Presbyterian churches. As the new curriculum came off the presses, more and more non-OP congregations began to use the work of Great Commission Publications. By 1971 the entire curriculum had been produced—a grade 1 through 12 sequence—and the number of non-OP churches using it totaled 435. The OPC itself in 1972 included approximately 140 congregations, 133 of which used this curriculum.

The size of the market outside the OPC, however, was still not sufficiently large to finance Great Commission Publications in full. By 1973 the debt for the Sunday school curriculum was a staggering $134,000. The need for an even larger outlet for the OPC materials was met in 1973, when conservatives in the Southern Presbyterian Church (PCUS) withdrew because of the rising tide of liberal theology in that denomination and formed the Presbyterian Church in America. At the very first PCA general assembly a committee met which included members of the OPC's Committee on Christian Education and whose task was to provide the framework for a joint publishing venture. By 1975 this goal became a reality. Great Commission Publications, which had been exclusively the publishing arm of the OPC's Committee on Christian Education, became the publisher of Christian education materials for both the OPC and the PCA. It is a corporation which includes six trustees (usually three ministers and three ruling elders) from each denomination. Such cooperative endeavors, no doubt, planted and watered the seeds for a merger between the OPC and PCA (see chapter nine). While the content of the material continued to be Reformed and biblically based, less prominent were tracts and publications which focused on the specific history and character of the OPC, a natural result of an agency which serves two denominations.

The new configuration of Great Commission Publications has freed the Committee on Christian Education to undertake other responsibilities. In 1980 the committee began to publish *New Horizons in the Orthodox Presbyterian Church*, the monthly news magazine for the denomination, filling a gap left in 1979 by the termination of the *Presbyterian Guardian*. The committee has also prepared materials and led seminars in the areas of worship, evangelism, fellowship, service, and Christian schooling. In addition, the Committee on Ministerial Training, historically a special committee of the general assembly which oversees the training of ministerial candidates, was in 1980 incorporated into the Committee on Christian Education.

Yet despite these newer efforts, the work of Christian education in the OPC still reflects the original vision that informed the founders of the denomination. The committee has been commited to the Reformed understanding of education. Christian education is not something just for Sunday school or only for ministers. It involves, like the Lordship of Christ, all areas of human knowledge and is required of all believers as a means of loving God, as Christ commanded, not just with our hearts and souls but also with our minds.

Assessment

The work of the OPC in the area of Christian education is no doubt impressive. For such a small denomination to undertake such a wide variety of materials and projects is indeed a tribute to the courageous leadership of many individuals, the willingness of church members to make financial sacrifices, and ultimately to God's faithfulness to his covenant people. Yet, the history all too briefly covered in this chapter raises a number of questions about the nature of Christian education and the way it has been practiced not just in the OPC but also within American Presbyterianism more generally.

One such question concerns the reliance upon Sunday school as a medium for instruction and the effect of this reliance on the institution of the family. Few American Presbyterians realize that Sunday school is a recent innovation within the history of Christianity. The Sunday school movement began around the time of the American revolution and was designed to instruct poor children in urban areas in the "three Rs"—reading, writing, and arithmetic. In other words, Sunday schools were originally concerned with so-called secular subjects, not with instruction in the Bible and doctrine. Over time, however, Sunday schools gradually assumed the form they have today. They provide a time on the Lord's Day where children learn about the Bible and the doctrinal teachings of the church. Given this history, one should be aware of the limits inherent to a Sunday school program. Obviously, the Sunday school cannot do the job alone, nor can it assume the responsibility of parents to raise their children in the fear and admonition of the Lord.

In fact, present difficulties in Christian education programs may stem from an overestimation of the importance of the Sunday school and an underestimation of the importance of the family. J. Gresham Machen himself traced the decline in biblical and theological knowledge within the Northern Presbyterian Church of his day to the decline of the family as a teaching institution and the neglect of the catechisms. He believed that denominational agencies, try as they might, finally were ineffective in educating church members, compared to the robust efforts of parents and families. To be sure, he believed that ministers and ruling elders were also responsible to instruct church members in the faith. But, as was true in his own experience, a lasting and meaningful education did not exist without the work of the family. The family, combined with a repeated and substantial acquaintance with the catechisms, Machen argued, was the best means of Christian education.

We who rely upon large-scale bureaucratic institutions such as schools, government, banks, hospitals, and chain stores for most of our basic needs tend to forget about the importance of the family.

But we need only to consider the prominence of the family in pre-modern societies, including the covenant community in the Scriptures, when the family performed almost all of the functions necessary for existence. Only with the rise of modern patterns of social organization has the task of Christian education shifted almost exclusively to the church. While the church has always had a responsibility to the covenant youth, i.e., to instruct them in the meaning of their baptism for proper participation in the Lord's Supper, it would do well to remember the experience and the practice of ancient societies.

If, as we now know, parents need to be involved with primary and secondary education for children to learn adequately, how much more is this the case with instruction in the Bible and doctrine? In fact, many sociological studies of twentieth-century Protestant families indicate that children are more likely to make a credible profession of faith and remain active in the church if their parents spend time instructing and talking to them about what they believe.

In addition to asking questions about the adequacy of Sunday school, we also need to examine the curriculum used by our churches. One of the hallmarks of the practices of Reformed and Presbyterian churches is catechesis. John Calvin as early as 1536, only three years after his conversion, produced a catechism for the youth in his congregation. Also, the Heidelberg Catechism (1563) served as the chief instructional aid for educating children in the Reformed churches of Europe. And the Westminster Assembly produced two catechisms, the Shorter and Larger. Yet the history of American Presbyterianism is one marked by remarkable silence about catechesis. Still, the Shorter and Larger Catechisms of the Westminster Assembly continue to rank among the best educational materials available, the former being designed for children and early teens, the latter for adults, young and old.

This is not meant in any way to diminish the accomplishments of the Committee on Christian Education or its publishing arm, Great Commission Publications. The substance of the materials produced by these agencies has been soundly Reformed and biblical. In fact, the OPC and GCP over the years have helped the church in the area of catechetical instruction—from Everett DeVelde's *Covenant Children's Catechumen Course*, to Dorothy

Partington Anderson's excellent catechetical course, *Bible Doctrine*, to Paul Settle's *Memory Work Notebook*, to the more recent efforts of Tom Tyson, general secretary for the Committee on Christian Education, to promote catechism instruction and memorization in the church. However, is it possible that catechesis could have an even more central and effective place in the OPC? This question the church may do well to consider.

11
Worship and the OPC

IT USED TO BE that spotting a Presbyterian worship service was a fairly easy task. Just as it was possible to identify a Roman Catholic service because of its mass, or an Anglican service because of its use of *The Book of Common Prayer*, so Presbyterian and Reformed worship was characterized by metrical psalm singing and expository preaching. But such brand name recognition is no more. Just as Roman Catholics have begun to experiment with guitar and polka masses, and as Episcopalians have begun to lift their hands into the air as much as they open their prayer books, so Presbyterians have started, as one publication has put it, to "expand their worship repertoire." On any given Lord's Day, Presbyterians will either be led in worship by their pastor or by a "worship team"; will sing praise to God either from hymnals or from overhead projections; will hear special music performed either by a robed choir or crooning singers and a rock band; and will either witness a short skit or sing a hymn to illustrate the point of the sermon.

The confusion of contemporary Presbyterian worship stems largely from the idea that worship is more or less a matter of taste, with the assumption being that there is no disputing about taste. Old forms of worship no longer seem plausible; they appear to be ineffective and, above all, boring. If we are going to retain our covenant youth and be effective in proclaiming the gospel in this culture, some argue, we need to keep pace and contextualize our message and worship, thereby making the Christian faith understandable to contemporary culture. And increasingly, effectiveness has come to mean abandoning a manner of worship that dates from the past and seems distant or alien. Many believe that as long as the content of our worship is sound, the form really does not matter. So the changes in worship appear merely to be alterations of form, dropping the style of an older generation for that of the boomers and busters.

Yet, the distinction so often drawn between form and content in worship appears to neglect the idea that theology and worship fit together like a hand in a glove. One Reformed scholar, G. van der Leeuw, has wisely observed that "whoever takes the little finger of liturgy soon discovers that he has grabbed the whole fist of theology." The point here is that it is impossible to divorce the form and content of worship. The tone and order of a worship service are not merely the husk of our theology but rather flow directly out of our conception of who God is and who we are as his people. So, for instance, if we take seriously the distinction between the Creator and creature that lies at the heart of biblical Christianity and the Reformed faith, how could the worship of Reformed believers ever suggest anything other than timidity, humility, and gratitude on the part of creatures? Along the same lines, if we think much about the doctrine of total depravity or original sin, with its implication that idolatry is the natural tendency of fallen men and women, will we ever try to devise God-honoring worship of our own making without consulting what Scripture says about how God desires to be worshiped? And if we are persuaded by the doctrine of divine sovereignty, would we ever tolerate a pattern of or practice in worship which implied that the triune God of Scripture was anything less than Lord of his church? Such questions demonstrate that the teachings of the Bible, as summarized in the Reformed faith, at countless points have a direct bearing on our worship. As T. David Gordon has written, "The distinctive principle of Presbyterian worship is nothing less than the consistent liturgical expression of its distinctive principles of theology, polity, and piety."

The Genius of Reformed Worship

An axiom of John Calvin's theology was the importance and centrality of worship for vital and genuine Christian faith and practice. In fact, Calvin put worship ahead of salvation in his list of the two most important facets of biblical religion. The Christian religion maintains its truth, he wrote, by "a knowledge, *first*, of the mode in which God is duly worshipped; and *secondly*, of the source from which salvation is to be obtained" (italics added). Calvin also observed that the first table of the law—the first four commandments—all directly related to worship, thus making worship "the first foundation of righteousness."

The prominence of worship in Calvin's theology led to his formulation of the *regulative principle*, one of the hallmarks of the Reformed tradition. This principle teaches that public worship is governed by God's revelation in his holy Word; whatever elements comprise corporate worship must be directly commanded by God in Scripture. The fact that a congregation has always worshiped in a particular way or that a certain practice stems from sincere piety are not sufficient reasons for ordering the worship service. According to Calvin, God not only "regards as fruitless, but also plainly abominates" whatever does not conform to his revealed will.

The regulative principle did not mean, as is sometimes alleged, that Calvin or others in the Reformed tradition advocated a set order of worship. Although Calvin followed a regular pattern in worship services at Geneva, he did not believe it was possible to prescribe all matters of worship. He acknowledged that there were incidental matters or circumstances (e.g., the time of the service, type of building, the use of pews) which Scripture did not determine. In such matters churches had freedom under the general guidelines of the Bible to implement practices that would honor God and edify his people. But Calvin did teach, and the Reformed tradition has maintained, that God does prescribe the elements of worship, that is, that preaching, prayer, the sacraments, songs of praise, and the reading of the Word are necessary to worship.

Not only did the desire to obey God inform Calvin's conception of the regulative principle, but just as important was the reformer's understanding of human depravity. The principle effect of Adam's first transgression was to turn all people into idolaters. All individuals, Calvin believed, even after the fall possessed a seed of religion, or a sense of God in their souls. But after the fall this religious sense no longer led to the true God but instead forced men and women to create gods of their own making, ones that conformed to their own selfishness and vanity. This temptation made

Calvin especially suspicious of practices in worship which were said to be pleasing or attractive to members of the congregation. He said, the more a practice "delights human nature, the more it is to be suspected by believers."

Even though Calvin and other Reformers hesitated to prescribe a specific liturgy for all churches, throughout western Europe from the sixteenth century until well into the eighteenth century there was remarkable agreement among Presbyterian and Reformed communions about the nature and manner of worship. The Westminster Assembly's Directory for Public Worship reflects that general consensus and is instructive for understanding the worship practices of the OPC. The assembly, which met from 1643 to 1648, is best known for the Westminster Confession of Faith and the Larger and Shorter Catechisms, documents which constitute the doctrinal standards of the OPC. Yet the assembly was charged with reforming all aspects of church life in Britain and so, in addition, it produced two documents with direct relevance to worship: a guide to corporate worship and a psalter.

The Directory for Public Worship carried forward many of the distinctive practices and convictions of Calvin regarding worship. Indeed, the directions for worship crafted by Reformed churches from Calvin's time up through that of the Westminster Assembly suggest several principles that have historically governed Presbyterians in worship. The first is the centrality of the Word of God. God's Word not only directs the form or manner of worship but also comprises the content of worship. It is read, sung, seen (in the Lord's Supper and baptism), and preached. The centrality of God's Word is especially evident in the Reformed emphasis upon preaching. In contrast to Roman Catholic worship where the focus is on the mass and the altar is the centerpiece of church architecture, the Reformers made preaching the central part of the service and put the pulpit front and center in the sanctuary.

A second principle of Reformed theology, very much related to the first, is that worship is theocentric. Worship is God-centered and its aim must be the glory of God. It is the highest form of fellowship between God and his people and must be done in spirit and truth. In fact, there is nothing that God hates more than false worship. Worship is absolutely necessary to Christian faith and practice, for God commands it and has so constituted us that worship is essential to the strengthening of our spiritual life.

The dialogical character of Reformed worship is the third principle. Corporate or public worship is the meeting of God with his people. Believers come at his invitation and are welcomed into his presence. God speaks through the call to worship, the reading of the Word, the sermon, and the benediction. Worshipers respond in song, prayer, and confession of faith.

The fourth principle of Reformed worship is simplicity. The fuller revelation of God in Christ in the new covenant means that Christians are not dependent on the childish and fleshly elements of the old covenant. Because of the work of Christ, believers already sit with him in glory, and this aspect of Christ's work greatly diminishes the church's need for visible or material supports in worship. Simplicity in worship, therefore, is closely related to spirituality. In the new covenant God is more fully present with his people than in the old covenant. But this presence is spiritual, not physical. Christ's command that his followers worship him in spirit and truth declares the new arrangement between God and his people.

The fifth and final principle of Reformed worship is reverence. According to Calvin, "pure and real religion" manifests itself through "faith so joined with an earnest fear of God that this fear also embraces willing reverence." Worship should be dignified and reverent, but it does not achieve these qualities through elaborate ceremonies or complex liturgies. In fact, Calvin believed that "wherever there is great ostentation in ceremonies, sincerity of heart is rare indeed." This does not mean that worship has no room for joy or emotion, as some critics of Reformed worship have charged. Joy, along with a full range of emotions—i.e., grief, anger, desire, hope, and fear—should be a part of worship. But the need for reverence and decorum dictates that any expression of emotion in worship should be tempered by modesty and self-control. And to insure that every aspect of worship is conducted decently and in good order, the Reformed tradition has insisted that every service be supervised by the elders, who bear responsibility for corporate worship, and that the minister, who speaks for God and for God's people, lead and direct the service.

American Developments

When Presbyterians migrated to the American colonies in the eighteenth century, there was some reservation about the Westminster Assembly's Directory for Public Worship. At the synod of 1729, for instance, the Presbyterian Church "recommended" the directory but was unwilling to take a stronger stand. The reason for this apparently cool reception was the desire to avoid another lengthy conflict like the one which had plagued the church over creedal subscription. But by 1786 the Synod "received" the directory "as in substance agreeable to the New Testament." And in 1788 the church adopted a revised directory that formed the basis for Presbyterian worship in America until the twentieth century.

Some changes in Presbyterian practice did make themselves evident following the Second Great Awakening, when American Presbyterians divided into New School and Old School parties. The Old School, the party which opposed the Arminian theology of revivals, stood for Puritan practices in worship. For them, every element in worship had to have biblical warrant (according to the regulative principle), and the service had to be characterized by decorum and solemnity. Worship for the Old School was an act that Christians directed toward God. In contrast, the New School, the party which promoted revivals, regarded worship more as a means to preach to and convert the lost. Consequently, the criterion for New School worship became evangelistic effectiveness, with the result that worship services began to look more like revival meetings. From the New School perspective, Old School worship was too intimidating to would-be Christians.

By the late nineteenth century, New School practices had been abandoned by most Presbyterians, but this did not mean the triumph of the Old School. While Presbyterian worship tended to be more formal, its formality reflected more the aesthetic tastes of polite society than the simplicity and reverence that had characterized Puritan and Old School worship. Choirs sang and organs played refined music, but the introduction of choirs and musical instruments into worship services were much debated matters, since they signaled a departure from worship convictions championed by Calvin and his followers.

The Practice of the OPC

When the OPC was founded, the church's instincts with re-gard to worship were clearly on the side of Calvin, the Puritans, and Old School Presbyterianism. Its reasons for breaking with the mainline church were precisely those which had an immediate bearing upon worship, namely, the regulative principle and theo-centric theology. The mainline church had substituted human ideas for the Word of God and had fashioned its message to win the approval of the surrounding culture rather than faithfully seek-ing to honor and glorify God.

The Directory for Public Worship adopted by the OPC's Sixth General Assembly (1939) reflected the new church's adherence to the theology of the Westminster Standards. Like the Westminster Assembly's directory, the OPC's contained no provisions for fu-neral or marriage services or the visitation of the sick. A number of pernicious notions had surrounded sickness, death, and mar-riage in Roman Catholicism, and the Reformers sought to purge these elements from ecclesiastical practice on the basis of the reg-ulative principle. The mainline Presbyterian Church had reintro-duced some of these practices into its directory for worship, but the OPC returned to the position of the Reformers.

In contrast to the mainline church's directory, which failed to include a theology of worship, the OPC supplied a helpful chapter on the principles of public worship. These principles repeat the in-sights of the Reformed tradition—the regulative principle, God's glory as the aim of worship, worship as an expression of faith in and love for Christ, the solemn and thankful character of worship, and worship as an activity for the covenant community. Also, as the Westminster divines had done, the committee which drafted the OPC's directory repeated the practice of including advice on how believers should sanctify the Lord's Day or Christian Sabbath, thus affirming the Puritan-American Presbyterian tradition of sabba-tarianism. Other chapters—there were only six in all—covered the other elements of Reformed worship: the parts of the worship service, the celebration of the sacraments, public profession of faith, and the ordination and installation of church officers.

One of the parts of public worship to which the OPC's direc-tory gave attention was congregational singing. As in the case of

Christian education materials, the new church found itself without recourse to a good hymnal or psalter. In 1933 the Presbyterian Church had issued a new hymnal to which conservatives objected, J. Gresham Machen among them, because of the liberal theology reflected in alterations of older hymns and in the new hymns which had been added. As early as 1943, the OPC appointed a committee to plan for the production of a hymnal. Another committee came before the church in 1946 and 1947 with reports on song in public worship, and in 1949 the general assembly created a committee with the responsibility of producing a hymnal. As committee member Edward J. Young wrote, the OPC "did not enter upon its task lightly."

The committee's reports of 1946 and 1947 which studied the use of song in public worship are worth some attention. The majority report, which won the approval of the general assembly in 1947, provided the rationale for the singing of hymns. But the differences between the majority and minority reports show how two centuries of American Presbyterian developments had brought change to original Reformed practice. The majority report on song (Kuiper, Marsden, E. J. Young, Skilton, and Kuschke) started in good Reformed fashion with a straightforward and full discussion of the regulative principle. Although the Westminster directory's understanding of the regulative principle commended metrical psalms as the content of congregational singing, the report refused to go in the direction of exclusive psalmody. It also said that there were certain areas of worship where the Bible allowed for the "exercise of a measure of liberty as regards the content of worship." This was especially true in the case of prayer. The Word of God did not stipulate "a set form of words" for prayers in worship, and because New Testament believers used hymns, the majority of the committee concluded that hymns theocentric in character, in addition to psalms, be used by OP congregations in worship.

The minority report, written by John Murray and William Young, argued for the exclusive use of psalms. It stated that the analogy between song and prayer drawn by the majority report was invalid; and in those cases where the church may not have sung Old Testament Psalms, they sang inspired verse. The conclusion Murray and Young drew was that the Bible authorized only the singing of "inspired songs," a conclusion which limited congregational singing to the Psalms and Scripture songs (i.e., the songs of Miriam, Hannah, Mary, Zechariah, and Simeon). These reports were sent to the presbyteries and sessions for study.

The *Trinity Hymnal*, which the OPC published in 1961, presented both psalms and hymns in accord with the majority committee report of 1947. There were 143 psalm versions, providing for a great expansion in OP use of psalms. This encouraged the congregations to implement the position of the OP Directory for Worship that the metrical versions of the Psalms "ought to be used frequently in public worship." Indeed, the hymnal was a monument to the theological sensitivities of the church, demonstrating the committee's commitment to present to the church hymns that were theologically sound and psalms and hymns that were singable.

The hymnal was arranged under four main headings—God, The Church, The Christian Life, and Occasional Hymns. The subject matter followed the order of topics covered in the Westminster Confession of Faith. By devoting separate sections to children's hymns and songs for informal occasions, the *Trinity Hymnal* also manifested the Reformed teaching that worship should be dignified and solemn. While some hymns may be useful for Sunday school, young people's meetings, or evangelistic services, these same songs are not necessarily appropriate for corporate worship. Thus the OPC's position on congregational singing, as expressed by the *Trinity Hymnal*, may be judged a balanced response to the issues raised by the minority in the church. Furthermore, the original hymnal provides a benchmark for all future efforts. The remarkable sale of this hymnal beyond the OPC was testimony that others recognized its tremendous value.

The Revisionist Impulse

Patterns of and ideas about worship for the first forty years of the OPC's history were, no doubt, fairly uniform and self-consciously Reformed, at least by North American standards. But in the last twenty years, efforts to change the worship practices of the denomination, spearheaded by the New Life movement and by the appeal of the charismatic movement, have been initiated. Throughout the 1980s, the OPC's Committee on Revisions to the

Book of Discipline and Directory for Public Worship proposed new chapters for the directory. As for the *Trinity Hymnal*, it was revised thoroughly by a new committee drawn from the PCA as well as from the OPC, a project accomplished in 1990 with the publication of the new *Trinity Hymnal*. While the proposed changes in the Directory of Worship and new hymnal continue to be informed by sound, biblical, Reformed insights and reflect the OPC's persistent commitment to traditional Presbyterian forms of worship, the process of revision also belies genuine discontent within the denomination about worship. This discontent was best summarized in the report to the Fifty-Fifth General Assembly (1989) about the Directory for Public Worship:

> There is widespread dissatisfaction or at least widespread lack of use in the OPC of the present Directory. There are parts of the present Directory that are so dated (e.g., "the stately rhythm of the choral") that there must be a rather thorough revision. Yet there is no consensus of where the church wants to go in worship. The current situation in the church regarding worship is diverse from near liturgical anarchy to others who feel that singing uninspired hymns is a violation of the regulative principle.

Other pressures on the worship practice of the OPC have come from two fronts. The first concerns the role of the laity in public worship. In the late 1980s, questions about certain congregations using women and non-ordained men in the leading of public worship provoked controversy in both the Presbyteries of the Midwest and Ohio. In the specific case of the Presbytery of Ohio, the worship policy of Covenant OPC, Pittsburgh, allowing women "to read the Scriptures, give encouragement from the Word, sing, participate in musical events and lead prayer in public worship" prompted members of the congregation in 1986 to complain to the session. Initially the debates focused on the permissibility of women to lead public worship, and both sides offered different interpretations of I Corinthians 11 and 14. The one side argued that the apostle Paul's clear teaching in the latter passage and in I Timothy 2 against women speaking in public worship should be the context for understanding I Corinthians 11, where he writes about women praying and prophesying. The session of Covenant Church, however, believed such exegesis was forced and thought that Paul's teaching in I Corinthians 11 should qualify the apostle's prohibitions against women speaking in public worship. When the session denied the complaint in 1987, an appeal went to the Presbytery of Ohio.

While the debate appeared to be leading to a consideration of whether women should be ordained in order to lead in worship, the committee appointed by the presbytery to report on the matter recognized that questions about the nature of corporate worship were also at stake. Over the course of the next two years presbytery tried to resolve the matter, but with little success. Problems delaying the adjudication of the matter concerned procedural questions (was the original complaint worded properly?), the practice of other OP congregations (whose worship policies were similar to those of Covenant Church), and ultimately a lack of consensus about the nature of worship and the participation of non-ordained church members in it. During these debates the presbytery heard careful exegesis of I Corinthians 11–14, sound appeals to the Directory for Public Worship, and strained arguments about the responsibility of gifted church members to encourage each other. The lack of consensus was so great that the presbytery actually reversed itself a couple of times—initially voting to sustain part of the complaint (which would have prohibited women from leading worship), then in the fall of 1988 voting to deny the complaint, and then upon appeal deciding at its spring 1989 meeting to sustain the complaint.

Uncertainties like these in the Presbytery of Ohio prompted the Fifty-Fifth General Assembly (1988) to appoint a committee to study the involvement of "unordained persons (men and women)" in the "regular worship service of the church." This committee produced three reports which it delivered to the general assembly three years later. The majority report (Gaffin, Jerrell, and Peterson) argued for the involvement of the unordained. Its position was that the regulative principle does not prohibit such involvement, that the involvement of the unordained should balance Paul's command that worship be done "decently and in order" (I Cor 14:40), and that such participation be done for the edification of the saints (I Cor 14:12). And, while recognizing that the assembly should not prescribe one policy for the whole church, the majority report did raise reservations about whether Presbyterian worship, if led only by the ordained, would be overly formal and ultimately sacerdotal, or priestly.

The minority reports argued for limiting the leadership of worship to the ordained. The first (Dennison) offered a careful history and interpretation of the Westminster Assembly's Directory for Public Worship and the OPC's directory in contending that only ministers should lead public worship. It observed that many of the changes surrounding worship in the OPC departed from Reformed exegetical principles, moved the denomination in the direction of evangelical and charismatic practices and theology, defined the nature of special office in functional rather than formal terms, and deviated from the traditional Presbyterian understanding of the regulative principle. The other minority report (Campbell) argued that only qualified men may lead in worship, thus allowing for qualified ruling elders to assist ministers. It made helpful points about the nature of congregational participation in worship even when they are not noticeably active, and went to great lengths to explain and defend the collective or corporate character of covenant worship.

The church took no action on the reports beyond referring them to the committee responsible for revising the Directory for Public Worship. But if these reports are any indication of the mind of the OPC on worship, it does appear that there is no consensus in the church on such matters, and that what has made Presbyterian worship historically distinctive is in danger of being abandoned. It does seem difficult to ignore the effects of popular culture and the increasing popularity of the charismatic movement on Presbyterian convictions about worship. The desire for entertainment as a chief reason for which people gather today, the demand for greater participation and expressiveness by "the people" in American culture more generally, and the influence of evangelical and charismatic worship through television and radio are factors which have undoubtedly contributed to much of the second-guessing about worship in the OPC.

To be sure, the genius of the Reformation was to repudiate any notion of holding on to tradition for tradition's sake. But while it is clear that the Reformed tradition is more difficult to defend, it is not clear that it has been bested by its rivals. Nor does it seem wise to make concessions in the area of worship while still trying to maintain and defend the other elements of the Reformed system, since much of the exegesis and argumentation undergirding Presbyterian convictions about worship are also the foundation for such doctrines as God, man, the covenant, salvation, and the church. The question needs to be asked whether it is possible to change one aspect of Presbyterian practice without also affecting the larger set of convictions.

Another area in which the "revisionist" impulse in worship has been felt in the OPC is that of Sabbath-keeping. The Westminster Confession of Faith states simply (21.7) that the Sabbath is to be "kept holy unto the Lord," the whole time being taken up "in the public and private exercises of his worship, and in the duties of necessity and mercy." Until this century, much of American Protestantism observed the Sabbath as the Westminster Confession described it. In our century, however, Sabbath-keeping has largely disappeared as a discipline of the Christian life for several reasons. With the rise of leisure activities and professional sports events there is a greater number of things competing for the Christian's attention. Indeed, the very term "weekend" is a modern one that suggests that both Saturday and Sunday are one run-on period of personal relaxation. Furthermore, the discipline of Sabbath-keeping is foreign to a culture that prizes freedom and spontaneity. Many churches have accommodated by offering several worship services, permitting attenders to choose that day and time that fits their lifestyle.

Generally this decline has not characterized the OPC. Most, though not all, OP congregations conduct both morning and evening worship services on the Lord's Day, bucking the trend to abandon the latter. Increasingly, evening service is emerging as an OP distinctive. The OPC Directory for Worship states that "the whole [Sabbath] day must be kept holy unto the Lord." Evening service is a vital tool for following that directive: together with the morning service, it frames the whole day around worship and draws it to a fitting conclusion by bringing together the people of God out of this world and into sanctuary with their God.

On one occasion the OPC engaged in extended debate on the Sabbath. In 1968 the Presbytery of Wisconsin, in the midst of a discipline case over the Rev. Francis Breisch's view of the Sabbath, overtured the general assembly, requesting that the church "evaluate the teachings of the Westminster Standards concerning the Sabbath." That assembly declined, however, to render a decision apart from an appeal from a presbytery decision. An appeal would come in the very next year in the form of a complaint entered against the Presbytery of Wisconsin for its failure to discipline Breisch. In response, the assembly appointed a Committee on Sabbath Matters.

In 1973 that committee presented a divided report. The majority report essentially upheld the complaint against the presbytery, denying that the Old Testament Sabbath was a ceremonial practice that was abolished by the work of Christ, and reaffirming the Lord's Day as the Christian Sabbath. It concluded that a minister's ordination vows in the OPC required a commitment to the teaching of the Westminster Standards regarding the Sabbath. A minority report took strong exception to this conclusion. The offenses alleged in the trial before the Presbytery of Wisconsin were not, it argued, "contrary, on any construction, to the Reformed system of doctrine." It went on to recommend that the general assembly "elect a committee to revise the teaching of our Standards regarding the Fourth Commandment." The 1973 Assembly determined to accept the recommendation of the majority report, thus refusing to revise the doctrine of the Sabbath found in the Westminster Confession.

To be sure, debates about the Sabbath some twenty years old are not necessarily the best indication of current practices in the OPC as it heads toward its sixtieth anniversary. Yet, if the church is continuing to hold the line on Sabbath observance—a remarkable feature in itself, since few Presbyterian churches today think twice about the uniqueness of the Lord's Day—then there is reason to hope that the OPC will also continue to preserve the distinctive character of Reformed worship. For ideas about worship and the Sabbath mutually reinforce each other and also water the soil from which the Reformed faith grows. At the heart of Reformed worship has always been the conviction that when believers gather on the Lord's Day, their practices should reflect their confession of faith. In worship we come before the holy and transcendent one, who is the righteous judge of the universe, whom we offend daily, and who has miraculously provided a way of salvation through his son, Jesus Christ. Worship should be a reminder of the gulf between God and sinners and of what he has done to overcome that gulf, lest believers lapse into a false understanding of God.

In sum, worship always reflects a church's theology. True theology yields true and acceptable worship. Improper or erroneous theology yields false worship. Worship is not a matter of taste; it is a statement of theological conviction. At its best, the OPC has followed this logic. By God's grace may it continue to do so, not for the sake of favorite hymns, traditional prayers, alternative music, or packed pews, but rather for the glory of our sovereign and saving God.

12
The Social Witness of the Church

BY ANY RECKONING, the 1960s and 1970s were traumatic decades for American evangelicalism. The encroaching effects of secularism and humanism, manifested in the rise of pornography, drug abuse, homosexuality, violent crime, and abortion-on-demand, crushed any consensus on "Judeo-Christian values" that might have previously existed. Together these evils galvanized conservative Christians to rethink the direction of American society and God's purposes for it. What was the witness-bearing role of the church in an increasingly secular culture? For most evangelicals, the answer was greater social engagement. In an attempt to recover lost ground, prominent fundamentalists like Jerry Falwell and Pat Robertson led their followers on aggressive social crusades, programs that ironically mirrored the liberal social gospel that fundamentalists had so often criticized. Fundamentalism and evangelicalism suddenly shifted from world-denying subcultures into movements committed to cultural transformation.

At the same time, subtle yet significant changes in leadership were taking place in the OPC, as many of the church's original ministerial members died or retired from active service. This is most clearly seen in changes at Westminster Theological Seminary. In 1960 the Westminster faculty still included five members who had been a part of the school since its early days and who were longtime ministers in the OPC: John Murray, Ned Stonehouse, Cornelius Van Til, Paul Woolley, and E. J. Young. All of these professors had been active in the affairs of the church, but by the mid-seventies they were gone from the seminary either by death or retirement.

How would the OPC respond to the cultural dislocations of the sixties and seventies? Would a change in leadership signal a new engagement in social reform? Response to the growing culture war in America was not a mere academic exercise for some churches. In 1979 the OP congregation in San Francisco was called to the front lines. When the church fired its organist, who was a professed homosexual, it was sued for violating the city's gay rights ordinance. Pastor Chuck McIlhenny described the ensuing litigation in this way: "Two diametrically opposed religions had clashed in the courtroom: secular humanism, the religion of our dominant culture, and orthodox Christianity." Defending itself on the basis of its First Amendment right of religious freedom, the church eventually won its long and expensive legal battle, but McIlhenny, his family, and the church have had to endure constant threats from gay rights activists ever since.

In light of these changes in the cultural landscape, many in the OPC would propose a more aggressive role in social activism. From 1986 to 1991, Grace OPC in Lynchburg, Virginia, published *Journey* Magazine. Edited by Richard Knodel, the church's minister, *Journey* was a combination of Calvinist orthodoxy and right-wing political ideology, deeply influenced by theonomy or "Christian Reconstruction." Theonomy holds that the Old Testament civil law was not unique to the theocracy of Israel but represents God's will for all nations at all times. Thus it sees the church as an instrument for reconstructing within contemporary culture an Old Testament-styled theocracy. God's blessing, theonomists believe, will come only to the nation obedient to biblical law. R. J. Rushdoony, regarded as the founder of the theonomic movement, was once an OP minister but he left the church in 1970. Another prominent theonomist, Greg Bahnsen, is an OP minister in southern California, where he directs a Christian study center.

Overall, however, *Journey*, theonomy, and other like-minded efforts have exercised limited influence on the denomination's thinking. Nor has the church joined the social crusading bandwagon of American evangelicalism. Instead, it has defined itself in distinction from this trend. Two pivotal commitments have helped shape the OPC's direction: the doctrines of the "spirituality of the church" and sphere sovereignty.

The Spirituality of the Church and Sphere Sovereignty

One of the differences that emerged between Southern and Northern Presbyterianism in the nineteenth century was the role of the church in public affairs. Much of Northern Presbyterianism, influenced by the success of social reform movements like abolition, was of a politically active mindset. Southern Presbyterians, by contrast, generally held that the church in its corporate capacity had no right or responsibility to engage in social reforms. Contending that both the rule and the weapons of the church were spiritual, advocates of the Southern position insisted on maintaining the "spirituality of the church."

Born and raised in the South, Machen was strongly influenced by the Southern Presbyterian tradition. Moreover, as a civil libertarian, he had little patience with the idealism and Victorian piety that characterized both liberals and fundamentalists in the North. Not all of his supporters, however, shared his political and cultural views. As we saw in chapter three, divisions on social issues partly caused the 1937 exodus of Carl McIntire and fundamentalists from the OPC.

That split would not empty the OPC of social reformers. In 1941 several commissioners, led by Edwin Rian, persuaded the Eighth General Assembly to appoint a Committee of Nine in part to map out a social agenda for the OPC. Its mandate was "to study the relationship of the OPC to society in general, and to other ecclesiastical bodies in particular" in order to suggest "ways and means whereby the message and methods of our church may be better implemented to meet the needs of this generation," and that the church "may have an increasing area of influence and make a greater impact on life today."

This committee's ambitious agenda was born of Rian's particular vision for the OPC. In order to be the spiritual successor of the Presbyterian Church in the USA, the OPC had to become culturally significant. Rian was disappointed in the results of the church's first five years, and this committee, he hoped, would set it back on the right track.

Cornelius Van Til and Murray F. Thompson co-authored a minority report. They recognized the valid intention of the committee to make the church's witness more effective. But they went on to express sharp criticism of this "super committee": "There is no part of the work of the church which can not be investigated and appraised by the Committee of Nine." They labeled such centralization of power as "bureaucratic and unpresbyterian." The minority also feared a relaxation of the OPC's "vigorous proclamation of our distinctive faith." Swayed by the minority report, the assembly discontinued the Committee of Nine.

Closely allied with the doctrine of the "spirituality of the church" in Reformed thinking is the idea of "sphere sovereignty." Formally developed by Abraham Kuyper, the Dutch Calvinist theologian and statesman, sphere sovereignty asserts that God exercises his sovereign lordship over all spheres of life. "There is not one square inch of the entire creation," Kuyper wrote, "about which Jesus Christ does not cry out, 'This is mine! This belongs to me!' " Because God alone is sovereign, human authority is limited and is derived from God. God delegates authority to the social structures that he has ordained (the family, the church, and the state), and each sphere's authority is limited to that realm of life which God intended it to regulate. No structure may transgress its sphere and lord it over another. Therefore, just as the church has particular tasks to perform—i.e., preaching, the sacraments, and discipline—so there are also specific duties which are to be carried out only by the state or the family.

The OPC's relative silence about social and political matters should not be read as an indication of indifference toward social issues but rather as respect for sphere sovereignty. While the church is not to be a political pressure group, individual political activity is a biblically permissible means for achieving social change. Indeed, the *Presbyterian Guardian* frequently exhorted its readers on the importance of active citizenship. Paul Woolley distinguished between the corporate church and the individual believer in an article in *Christianity Today* with the provocative title, "Reinforcing the Wall Between Church and State":

> The Bible teaches that faith in God is the foundation for all attempts to meet human need. The Christian Church meets the spiritual needs of men. It teaches them how to face their own relation

to God, and it teaches them how the grace of God operates. When that grace has worked in the heart of a man, he becomes concerned about human need. As a Christian citizen he, not the church, goes out to do battle with the social ills of men. The Christian must battle social ills. The church tells him so. They must be fought, and fought on Christian principles. But it is the citizen, not the church, who goes to the war.

Neither the "spirituality of the church" nor sphere sovereignty render the church completely silent on social matters, however. The Westminster Confession speaks of a "humble petition" whereby the church can address the state without transgressing its sphere of responsibility: "Synods and councils are to handle, or conclude nothing, but that which is ecclesiastical: and are not to intermeddle with civil affairs which concern the commonwealth, unless by way of humble petition in cases extraordinary" (31.4). On a few occasions the OPC contemplated entering public debate by way of humble petition. For example, in 1960 a resolution was put to the floor of the general assembly urging American citizens not to vote for a Roman Catholic candidate for the presidency of the United States on the grounds that the Vatican is "a foreign power seeking control of the United States." The assembly eventually defeated this resolution. On other occasions humble petitions were made. In 1965 the assembly adopted a resolution against a proposal before the United States Senate to hold national elections on Sunday. In 1993 the general assembly petitioned President Clinton not to remove the ban against homosexuals in the military.

In that same 1993 Assembly, a debate arose over the nature and extent of "humble petitions." The assembly was asked to evaluate the propriety of a lawsuit that the Presbytery of New Jersey had filed against the State of New Jersey when the state passed a homosexual civil rights bill. The presbytery eventually persuaded the assembly that acting as a plaintiff in court could be interpreted as a "humble petition" in an extraordinary case. A minority filed a protest challenging that logic and lamenting the presbytery's "direct and aggressive approach to the state" that resembled "the political activism of both New School presbyterianism and fundamentalism." It remains to be seen which way the church will go on this issue.

One of the most significant studies on social matters that the OP general assembly commissioned had to do with abortion. In the wake of increasingly liberalized abortion laws, the 1970 General Assembly appointed a Committee to Study the Matter of Abortion. The committee submitted its report the next year. The report cautioned against a simplistic interpretation of Scripture and asserted that one cannot prove from the Scriptures that a fetus is a human being from the point of conception. But it went on to argue that the Bible taught a continuity between fetal and post-natal life. The burden of proof, the report concluded, fell on those who sought to find a biblical distinction between a person and a fetus, a distinction necessary to permit abortion.

Paul Woolley, in a minority report, located the burden of proof elsewhere. It was not clear, he argued, that a pre-born is a human being, and the Bible does not teach that the taking of such life is murder. If God has not prohibited an action, the church must not do so, or else it speaks beyond the teaching of the Bible.

Both reports were sent to the presbyteries for their recommendations and review. In the next year the general assembly passed a statement on abortion that read in part, "voluntary abortion, except possibly to save the physical life of the mother, is in violation of the Sixth Commandment."

Social Justice within the Church

Beyond the occasional proclamation to society at large, the church has also sensed the need to provide guidance to its own members on social issues. Three recent concerns have been race relations, the principles of diaconal ministry, and the role of women in the church.

OPC discussions of race relations generally arose through its involvement in the Reformed Ecumenical Synod. Throughout the years of its membership in the RES, the OPC had voiced concern over the practice of apartheid in the member churches in South Africa. In 1952, acting on an overture from the Presbytery of Philadelphia, the general assembly requested that the RES, in its 1953 meeting, inquire of the South African churches if they support the government policy of apartheid, and if so, how they reconcile it with the teachings of the Bible. In 1983 the OPC sent a pastoral letter to South African churches urging them "not to live by standards and practices of the world but by the renewing power of the Holy Spirit."

Early in the 1970s the RES sponsored a series of Regional Conferences on Race. One that was held in Chicago in 1971 reached a series of conclusions that drew fire in the OPC for its social agenda, including recommendations that the member churches promote political and economic justice, provide legal aid for the poor, and combat housing discrimination. The *Presbyterian Guardian* lampooned the conference as a "hodge-podge of social do-goodism." At the general assembly that summer, several commissioners protested against the "methodologies of the social gospel" behind the conference that were unscriptural and "therefore inimical to the Reformed faith." In response, the assembly commissioned a Committee on the Problem of Race with the task of equipping the OPC with alternative proposals. Its report in 1974 consisted of a set of general suggestions, from maintaining Reformed witnesses in urban areas, to encouraging presbyteries and sessions to engage in seasons of prayer and in regional conferences on the problems of race.

The second concern the denomination has addressed is its diaconal ministry. At the 1947 General Assembly, the OPC established its Committee on Diaconal Ministry (then called the Committee on General Benevolence). From its inception, a priority of this committee has been the care of retired ministers and widows of deceased ministers. Among the sacrifices that these men made in joining the OPC was the loss of their insurance and pension benefits, and special funds were established to meet those needs. The committee also ministered to OP members whose physical needs exceeded the provisions of local church diaconates, and it served Christians beyond the OPC, especially working with the church's foreign missions.

But beyond ministering to Christians, what role does the diaconate play? As we saw in chapter six, this issue was partially addressed by the 1964 General Assembly when it approved the establishment of medical missionary work in Eritrea. Desiring a fuller study of that issue, the 1980 General Assembly appointed a Committee to Study the Principles of Diaconal Ministry, which presented divided conclusions to the 1984 Assembly. Both reports affirmed the covenantal emphasis of diaconal work (we must do good first to the "household of faith") and both refused to limit mercy ministries *only* to Christians. Yet they differed on the extent of aid to the non-Christian. The majority argued that "diaconal mercy is unlimited in that it seeks to reach out in Christ's name to all types of needy people in all types of situations." In his minority report, Leonard Coppes was more restrictive. Christian mercy, he argued, does not extend to all the poor and needy of the world, but temporary help may be provided only to the non-Christians "in dire need and within the immediate proximity of [the covenant] community." The assembly determined to send both reports to the churches for study.

The third social concern that the OPC has addressed is the role of women in the church. Throughout the history of American evangelicalism, women have played significant roles in the creative use of their gifts, and women in the OPC have been no exception. Increasingly, however, voices of "biblical feminism" have questioned whether evangelical churches have frustrated women from the full use of their gifts by barring them from ordained offices in the church. They have argued that traditional interpretations of Pauline texts such as 1 Timothy 2:12 have misunderstood the cultural setting of an argument that was not intended as a universal principle for the church.

In 1979 the Bethel OPC in Wheaton, Illinois, submitted an overture to the Presbytery of the Midwest requesting that it "establish a special committee to study the biblical teaching of the role of women in the church and to consider its implications for the ordination of women to church office." Eventually Bethel's overture was sent to the general assembly, which in 1984 appointed a Committee on the Hermeneutics of Women in Office.

The next year the committee presented a provocative report that challenged the church to examine the historical and cultural assumptions it brought to the issue of women in office: "Could it be," the report asked, "that we are simply too accustomed to the idea of exclusively male leadership and to the notion that such a position alone is compatible with a high view of Scripture?" The committee's intention was not to question the OPC's position on women's ordination but to urge the church not to assume that its view is the only consistent biblical position. In other words, the committee sought to frame the issue in terms of biblical interpretation. The assembly was clearly uncomfortable with the approach of the committee, and it took the unusual step of excluding its report from the assembly's minutes.

The next year a reconstituted committee focused more narrowly on the question of women in the diaconate. Affirming the biblical teaching that excludes women from the offices of minister and elder, the committee was split on the office of deacon, with one member arguing for the legitimacy of women deacons. The assembly sent both reports to presbyteries and sessions for study, but by this time the Wheaton church was deeply divided. Complaints were brought to two assemblies against actions of the session which had moved in the direction of women in office. The complaints were sustained. By 1989, over half the church left to form a congregation in the Evangelical Presbyterian Church, a denomination open to women's ordination.

A Committee on Church and Society?

Perhaps the most ambitious attempts to engage the church in discussions of social witness began in 1987, when the Fifty-Fourth General Assembly established a special committee to explore the feasibility of a permanent committee on public religious matters. In its report, submitted to the Fifty-Seventh Assembly in 1990, the special committee contended that the historical reluctance of the church to discuss social issues was not "strong enough to resist the need of the church to speak to its own people and/or to the increasingly non-Christian society in which we live, after the manner of the prophets." And so it proposed the establishment of a Committee on Church and Society.

Challenging the assumption that the Church may not address "public religious" issues, the report argued:

"Indeed, there may be instances in which the Church *must* so speak. The church has the right and responsibility to teach its own membership the whole counsel of God. That whole counsel includes Christ's claims on social issues. The notion of a church that teaches the principles of political action but refrains from interfering as a church in the political process should not provoke fears of content-less posturing or of abandoning hope of action. It is simply a recognition of the inseparability of the cultural mandate and the Great Commission."

In proposing a Committee on Church and Society, the report was suggesting ways in which the OPC might express the social implications of the gospel in more effective and efficient ways than it had in the past. It was wary of the pitfalls of its proposals, and it urged the church to steer a careful course between pietism and activism. Moreover, its carefully crafted purpose suggested none of the bureaucratic power of the Committee of Nine.

Yet the report failed to overcome challenges of a minority report and of the assembly's Advisory Committee. Together, these dissenters preferred that the general assembly address social issues occasionally, and only in the context of a judicial case. Further, they objected that the proposed committee would entail the church adopting, in effect, official interpretations of the church's confessional standards. The minority report also warned the church to maintain the primacy of preaching in its social witness: "When the church in Acts turned the world upside down, it did that not by advising Pilate how to rule Palestine, but by preaching the gospel." The committee's recommendation, it feared, was ultimately "a distraction from the church's primary task of preaching to a dying culture." The assembly acted on the recommendation of the minority report and did not establish a Church and Society Committee.

The OPC: A Pilgrim People

Throughout its history, the OPC has struggled with defining its task to be salt and light to a post-Christian culture. In contrast to the transformationist vision of other conservative denominations, the OPC, in the words of historian Charles Dennison, "has no cultural or social agenda. She resisted every attempt to so define her." The church resisted the Committee of Nine's effort to so define her in 1942, and it declined to establish a Committee on Church and Society nearly fifty years later. This dissent is often viewed as social indifference, and perhaps it helps to account for the church's lack of popularity.

This mindset has other theoretical foundations beyond Machen's view of the spirituality of the church or Kuyper's sphere sovereignty. The apologetic methodology of Cornelius Van Til, as we saw in chapter seven, stressed the radical antithesis between believers and the world. Under Van Til's influence, the church has sought to maintain its purity against the threats of paganism, an emphasis that tempers a culture-transforming agenda. The chasm between the way that believers and non-believers think means, in part, that the church should not expect (nor persuade) a godless culture to emulate Christian ways apart from acknowledging Christ as Savior and Lord.

The church is also influenced by the hermeneutical insights of Geerhardus Vos, professor of Biblical Theology at Princeton Theological Seminary from 1893 to 1932 (where he taught Kuiper, Machen, Murray, Stonehouse, and Van Til). Vos's pioneering work highlighted the organic character of the progressive revelation of the Bible, especially the "already/not yet" paradox of the coming of the kingdom in the death and resurrection of Christ. In Vos's understanding, the kingdom and its blessings are "already" present in believers: in their union with Christ they have died, and their life is "hidden with Christ in God" (Col 3:3). Yet the kingdom is "not yet" here in its fullest and most glorious form; this awaits the second advent of Christ. The Christian life is a pilgrim experience, fulfilling its calling while anticipating its final destination. Vos's teaching was fully in line with John Calvin's statement that "it is a Judaic folly to look for the kingdom of Christ among the things that make up this world, and to shut it up among them." Calvin went on to write that the "plainest" teaching of Scripture is that "the fruit we reap from grace is spiritual fruit" (*Institutes*, IV. xx. 1). In other words, the kingdom of God cannot be located in the politics or social arrangement of the United States. Rather, we look for that kingdom in the work of the church and in the sanctification of believers.

In stark contrast with this Reformed understanding of the kingdom of God, American evangelicals are prone to judge the success of the church in terms of its influence in the world. Accordingly, some of the OPC's evangelical critics have often dismissed the church as "irrelevant" for its want of a social agenda. Seen from another perspective, however, it is more accurate to say that the OPC is committed to the "irrelevance" of the world to the church. As part of the new eschatological order unveiled in the coming of Christ, the church locates its hope in a kingdom that is not of this world, a kingdom that cannot be shaken. For that source of solid hope and comfort the OPC abandons aspiration for earthly glory, including a "restorationism" that yearns for a return to Judeo-Christian values, a theocratic state, or Christian civilization. Instead, the church longs and waits patiently for the return of Christ at his second coming, when his reign will be completely realized.

Theologian Richard B. Gaffin, Jr., in reflecting on the theological identity of the OPC, likens the church to Israel in its wilderness experience. Like Israel, the church has been delivered from bondage, but it has not yet entered the promised land. Like Israel, the church is traveling toward its Sabbath-rest (Heb 4:9). "In journeying to its final destination," Gaffin says, "the church confesses that it is a company of pilgrims, a people on the way. We do not have here an abiding city. We are looking for that city to come. Along the way we are exposed to testing and temptation, to all sorts of mirages and false hopes that inevitably attract the desert traveler. To be faithful to God, the church must maintain its heavenly vision. It must refuse to locate its hope in its desert experience. As the church worships and serves God in the desert, it will go from strength to strength." And, we might add, from glory to glory.

Conclusion:
The OPC and the Future

WHAT THEN about the future? The preceding pages have re-vealed a church attempting under difficult circumstances, and not always successfully, to maintain and perpetuate the Reformed faith, not out of loyalty to any particular individual but because of a desire to proclaim the whole counsel of God as revealed in Scrip-ture. The OPC's commitment to the Reformed faith is in fact the thing that makes the church unique. While other churches also endeavor to proclaim and apply the truths of the Westminster Confession of Faith and Catechisms, the OPC's commitment to these doctrinal standards has been different and more rigorous than most other Presbyterian communions.

Whatever the assessment of the OPC's theology and practice, here is its distinguishing mark. During the struggles of the funda-mentalist-modernist controversy, those leaders who would even-tually found the OPC stood firmly against not only the dangers of liberalism but also the mainline Presbyterian Church's failure to maintain a credible Reformed witness. And since its founding in 1936, the OPC has strived to be obedient to the teaching of God's Word as summarized in the Westminster Confession of Faith and Catechisms. From the way it has planted churches both at home and abroad, to the way it has pursued relations with other Protes-tant bodies and groups, to the way it has understood and carried out the work of the institutional church, the OPC has demonstrat-ed a robust effort to live out the Reformed teachings that emerged during the heroic struggles of the sixteenth and seventeenth centuries, while seeking to ground those teachings in, and to verify them from, God's holy Word.

Some may wonder, however, whether the OPC has been as effective as it could have been. Indeed, when one considers the enormous challenges that the contemporary world poses for God's people, one may be tempted to conclude that new times demand new methods. We will always be committed to the truths of the Reformed faith, some may argue, but the way we propagate and communicate those truths may need to change according to the necessities of the times.

Yet, the origins and early history of the OPC remind us that the challenges which confronted the church's first generation were no less staggering than those encountered at the close of the twentieth century. To be sure, the OPC during its first two decades did not have to worry to the same degree that we do, for instance, about the effects of television, drugs, rapid social mobility, rising divorce rates, and the so-called sexual revolution, developments which have done as much to challenge the contemporary church's message as they have the expectations which modern men and women bring to the church. Nevertheless, the denomination was born at a time when many of these same forces were prompting Protestant leaders to rethink the witness and task of the church. The OPC did not originate during the halcyon days of rural America when the church stood at the center of community and family life. Rather, the OPC began at a time when the acids of modernity had already begun to eat away at the fabric of American society. In fact, the founding of the OPC was an explicit repudiation of mainline Protestantism's effort to refashion the gospel and the church's ministry in order to respond better to the perils of massive immigration, large impersonal cities, and economic chaos. In contrast to those Protestants who believed that the new age demanded a new message, a "social gospel" as it were, the OPC was dedicated to the idea that the old gospel of salvation in Christ was the only hope for sinners and that God ordained the church to do the special and glorious work of proclaiming that gospel.

This book can be read, therefore, as a warning against the temptation of every generation to think that its situation in history is peculiar and requires an exceptional or new remedy. Indeed, the history of the OPC demonstrates a remarkable record of resisting this way of thinking. The OPC has not let the fluctuations of politics, economics, and family life become distractions from the truths of the gospel or from the means God has appointed for gathering and preserving his people. This book also demonstrates that today's temptation to pursue a more effective or up-to-date strategy is not new. At times the OPC has been overwhelmed by the destructiveness and hollowness of modern life, and some of its members have contemplated pursuing a course that seemed better adapted to modern times. But by God's grace the church has recognized that the troubles of this life are swallowed up in the sweet communion God has with his people and that the church's task, no matter how irrelevant it may seem, is to make known the good news that God offers rest to the weary soul in the saving work of Christ Jesus.

For this reason we have chosen to conclude with an address by J. Gresham Machen, delivered in 1933 before the American Academy of Political and Social Science. The topic of that address was precisely this question of the church's relevance to modern life. What is that task of the church in modern times? Does the urgency of contemporary life require the church to pursue a new or different course? Machen's unusual answer to this question was the vision that motivated the OPC at its founding and has continued to inform the church throughout its relatively short history. And it is a message that, while reminding the OPC of its roots, also provides unparalleled guidance as the church seeks to be faithful and to fight the good fight on the brink of a new century.

The Responsibility of the Church in Our New Age

J. Gresham Machen

THE QUESTION of the church's responsibility in the new age involves two other questions: (1) What is the new age? (2) What is the church?

The former question is being answered in a number of different ways; differences of opinion prevail, in particular, with regard to the exact degree of newness to which the new age may justifiably lay claim. There are those who think that the new age is so very new that nothing that approved itself to past ages can conceivably be valid now. There are others, however, who think that human nature remains essentially the same and that two and two still make four. With this latter point of view I am on the whole inclined to agree. In particular, I hold that facts have a most unprogressive habit of staying put, and that if a thing really happened in the first century of our era, the acquisition of new knowledge and the improvement of scientific method can never make it into a thing that did not happen.

Such convictions do not blind me to the fact that we have witnessed astonishing changes in our day. Indeed, the changes have become so rapid as to cause many people to lose not only their breath but also, I fear, their head. They have led many people to think not only that nothing that is old ought by any possibility to remain in the new age, but also that whatever the new age favors is always really new.

Both these conclusions are erroneous. There are old things which ought to remain in the new age; and many of the things, both good and bad, which the new age regards as new are really as old as the hills.

In the former category are to be put, for example, the literary and artistic achievements of past generations. Those are things which the new age ought to retain, at least until the new age can produce something to put in their place, and that it has so far signally failed to do. I am well aware that when I say to the new age that Homer is still worth reading, or that the Cathedral of Amiens is superior to any of the achievements of the *art nouveau*, I am making assertions which it would be difficult for me to prove. There is no disputing about tastes. Yet, after all, until the artistic impulse is eradicated more thoroughly from human life than has so far been done even by the best efforts of the metallic civilization of our day, we cannot get rid of the categories of good and bad or high and low in the field of art. But when we pay attention to those categories, it becomes evident at once that we are living today in a drab and decadent age, and that a really new impulse will probably come, as it has come so many times before, only through a rediscovery of the glories of the past.

Something very similar needs to be said in the realm of political and social science. There, too, something is being lost—something very precious, though very intangible and very difficult of defense before those who have not the love of it in their hearts. I refer to civil and religious liberty, for which our fathers were willing to sacrifice so much. . . . Everywhere in the world we have centralization of power, the ticketing and cataloguing of the individual by irresponsible and doctrinaire bureaus, and, worst of all, in many places we have monopolistic control of education by the state.

But is all that new? In principle it is not. Something very much like it was advocated in Plato's *Republic* over two thousand years ago. The battle between collectivism and liberty is an age-long battle; and even the materialistic paternalism of the modern state is by no means altogether new. The technique of tyranny has, indeed, been enormously improved; a state-controlled compulsory education has proved far more effective in crushing out liberty than the older and cruder weapons of fire and sword, and modern experts have proved to be more efficient than the dilettante tyrants of the past. But such differences are differences of degree and not of kind, and essentially the battle for freedom is the same as it always has been.

If that battle is lost, if collectivism finally triumphs, if we come to live in a world where recreation as well as labor is prescribed for us by experts appointed by the state, if the sweetness and the sorrows of family relationships are alike eliminated and liberty becomes a thing of the past, we ought to place the blame for this sad denouement—for this sad result of all the pathetic strivings of the human race—exactly where it belongs. And it does not belong to the external conditions of modern life. I know that there are those who say that it does belong there; I know that there are those who tell us that individualism is impossible in an industrial age. But I do not believe them for one moment. Unquestionably, industrialism, with the accompanying achievements of modern science in both the physical and the social realm, does constitute a great temptation to destroy freedom; but temptation is not compulsion, and of real compulsion there is none.

No, my friends, there is no real reason for mankind to surrender to the machine. If liberty is crushed out, if standardization has its perfect work, if the worst of all tyrannies, the tyranny of the expert, becomes universal, if the finer aspirations of humanity give way to drab efficiency, do not blame the external conditions in the world today. If human life becomes mechanized, do not blame the machine. Put the blame exactly where it belongs—upon the soul of man.

Is it not in general within that realm of the soul of man that the evils of society have their origin today? We have developed a vast and rather wonderful machinery—the machinery of our modern life. For some reason, it has recently ceased to function. The experts are busily cranking the engine, as I used to do with my Ford car in the heroic days when a Ford was still a Ford. They are wondering why the engine does not start. They are giving learned explanations of its failure to do so; they are adducing the most intricate principles of dynamics. It is all very instructive, no doubt.

But the real explanation is much simpler. It is simply that the driver of the car has forgotten to turn on the switch. The real trouble with the engine of modern society is that it is not producing a spark. The real trouble lies in that unseen realm which is found within the soul of man.

That realm cannot be neglected even in a time of immediate physical distress like the present. I do not know in detail how this physical distress is to be relieved. I would to God that I did. But one thing I do know; it will never be relieved if, in our eagerness to relieve it, we neglect the unseen things. It is not practical to be merely practical men; man cannot successfully be treated as a machine; even the physical welfare of humanity cannot be attained if we make that the supreme object of our pursuit; even in a day when so many material problems are pressing for our attention, we cannot neglect the evils of the soul.

But if that be so, if the real trouble with the world lies in the soul of man, we may perhaps turn for help to an agency which is generally thought to have the soul of man as its special province. I mean the Christian church. That brings us to our second question: What is the church?

About nineteen hundred years ago, there came forth from Palestine a remarkable movement. At first it was obscure, but within a generation it was firmly planted in the great cities of the Roman Empire and within three centuries it had conquered the Empire itself. It has since then gone forth to the ends of the earth. That movement is called the Christian church.

What was it like in the all-important initial period, when the impulse which gave rise to it was fresh and pure? With regard to the answer to that question, there may be a certain amount of agreement among all serious historians, whether they are themselves Christians or not. Certain characteristics of the Christian church at the beginning stand out clear in the eyes both of friends and of foes.

It may clearly be observed, for example, that the Christian church at the beginning was radically doctrinal. Doctrine was not the mere expression of Christian life, as it is in the pragmatist skepticism of the present day, but—just the other way around—the doctrine, logically though not temporally, came first and the life afterward. The life was founded upon the message, and not the message upon the life.

That becomes clear everywhere in the primary documents. It appears, for example, in the first epistle to the Thessalonians, which is admitted by all serious historians, Christian and non-Christian, to have been really written by a man of the first Christian generation—the man whose name it bears. The apostle Paul there gives us a summary of his missionary preaching in Thessalonica—that missionary preaching which in Thessalonica and in Philippi and elsewhere did, it must be admitted, turn the world upside down. What was the missionary preaching like? Well, it contained a whole system of theology. "Ye turned to God," says Paul, "from idols to serve the living and true God, and to wait for His Son from heaven, whom He raised from the dead, even Jesus, which delivereth us from the wrath to come." Christian doctrine, according to Paul, was not something that came after salvation, as an expression of Christian experience, but it was something necessary to salvation. The Christian life, according to Paul, was founded upon a message.

The same thing appears when we turn from Paul to the very first church in Jerusalem. That too was radically doctrinal. In the first epistle to the Corinthians—again one of the universally accepted epistles—Paul gives us a summary of what he had received from the primitive Jerusalem church. What was it that he had received; what was it that the primitive Jerusalem church delivered over unto him? Was it a mere exhortation; was it the mere presentation of a program of life; did the first Christians in Jerusalem say merely: "Jesus has lived a noble life of self-sacrifice; we have been inspired by Him to live that life and we call upon you our hearers to share it with us?" Not at all. Here is what those first Christians said: "Christ died for our sins according to the Scriptures: He was buried; He has been raised on the third day according to the Scriptures." That is not an exhortation, but a rehearsal of facts; it is couched not in the imperative but in the indicative mood; it is not a program, but a doctrine.

I know that modern men have appealed sometimes at this point from the primitive Christian church to Jesus Himself. The primitive church, it is admitted, was doctrinal; but Jesus of Nazareth, it is said, proclaimed a simple gospel of divine Fatherhood and human brotherhood, and believed in the essential goodness of man. Such an appeal from the primitive church to Jesus used to be expressed in the cry of the so-called "Liberal" church, "Back to Christ!" But that cry is somewhat antiquated today. It has become increasingly clear to the historians that the only Jesus whom we find attested for us in our sources of information is the supernatural Redeemer presented in the four Gospels as well as in the epistles of Paul. If there was back of this supernatural figure a real, non-doctrinal, purely human prophet of Nazareth, his portrait must probably lie forever hidden from us. Such, indeed, is exactly the skeptical conclusion which is being reached by some of those who stand in the van of what is called progress in New Testament criticism today.

There are others, however—and to them the present writer belongs—who think that the supernatural Jesus presented in all of our sources of information was the real Jesus who walked and talked in Palestine, and that it is not necessary for us to have recourse to the truly extraordinary hypothesis that the intimate friends of Jesus, who were the leaders of the primitive church, completely misunderstood their Master's person and work.

Be that as it may, there is, at any rate, not a trace of any non-doctrinal preaching that possessed one bit of power in those early days of the Christian church. It is perfectly clear that that strangely powerful movement which emerged from the obscurity of Palestine in the first century of our era was doctrinal from the very beginning and to the very core. It was totally unlike the ethical preaching of the Stoic and Cynic philosophers. Unlike those philosophers, it had a very clearcut message; and at the center of that message was the doctrine that set forth the person and work of Jesus Christ.

That brings us to our second point. The primitive church, we have just seen, was radically doctrinal. In the second place, it was radically intolerant. In being radically intolerant, as in being radically doctrinal, it placed itself squarely in opposition to the spirit of that age. That was an age of synchronism and tolerance in religion; it was an age of what J. S. Phillimore has called "the courtly polygamies of the soul." But with that tolerance, with those courtly polygamies of the soul, the primitive Christian church would have nothing to do. It demanded a completely exclusive devotion.

A man could not be a worshiper of the God of the Christians and at the same time be a worshiper of other gods; he could not accept the salvation offered by Christ and at the same time admit that for other people there might be some other way of salvation; he could not agree to refrain from proselytizing among men of other faiths, but came forward, no matter what it might cost, with a universal appeal. That is what I mean by saying that the primitive Christian church was radically intolerant.

In the third place, the primitive church was radically ethical. Religion in those days, save among the Jews, was by no means closely connected with goodness. But with such a non-ethical religion the primitive Christian church would have nothing whatever to do. God, according to the primitive Christians, is holy; and in His presence no unclean thing can stand. Jesus Christ presented a life of perfect goodness upon earth; and only they can belong to Him who hunger and thirst after righteousness. Christians were, indeed, by no means perfect; they stood before God only in the merit of Christ their Savior, not in their own merit; but they had been saved for holiness, and even in this life that holiness must begin to appear. A salvation which permitted a man to continue in sin was, according to the primitive church, no matter what profession of faith it might make, nothing but a sham.

These characteristics of primitive Christianity have never been completely lost in the long history of the Christian church. They have, however, always had to be defended against foes within as well as without the church. The conflicts began in apostolic days, and there is in the New Testament not a bit of comfort for the feeble notion that controversy in the church is to be avoided, that a man can make his preaching positive without making it negative, that he can ever proclaim truth without attacking error. Another conflict arose in the second century, against Gnosticism, and still another when Augustine defended against Pelagius the Christian view of sin.

At the close of the Middle Ages, it looked as though at last the battle were lost—as though at last the church had become merged with the world. When Luther went to Rome, a blatant paganism was there in control. But the Bible was rediscovered; the ninety-five theses were nailed up; Calvin's *Institutes* was written; there was a counter-reformation in the church of Rome; and the essential

character of the Christian church was preserved. The Reformation, like primitive Christianity, was radically doctrinal, radically
intolerant, and radically ethical. It preserved these characteristics
in the face of opposition. It would not go a step with Erasmus, for
example, in his indifferentism and his tolerance; it was founded
squarely on the Bible, and it proclaimed, as providing the only way
of salvation, the message that the Bible contains.

At the present time, the Christian church stands in the midst
of another conflict. Like the previous conflicts, it is a conflict not
between two forms of the Christian religion but between the
Christian religion on the one hand and an alien religion on the
other. Yet—again like the previous conflicts—it is carried on
within the church. The non-Christian forces have made use of
Christian terminology and have sought to dominate the organization of the church.

This modern attack upon the Christian religion has assumed
many different forms, but everywhere it is essentially the same.
Sometimes it is frankly naturalistic denying the historicity of the
basic miracles, such as the resurrection of Jesus Christ. At other
times it assails the necessity rather than the truth of the Christian
message; but, strictly speaking, to assail the necessity of the message is to assail its truth, since the universal necessity of the message is at the center of the message itself. Often the attack uses the
shibboleths of a complete pragmatist skepticism. Christianity, it
declares, is a life and not a doctrine; and doctrine is the expression,
in the thought-forms of each generation, of Christian experience.
One doctrine may express Christian experience in this generation;
a contradictory doctrine may express it equally well in a generation
to come. That means, of course, not merely that this or that truth
is being attacked, but that truth itself is being attacked. The very
possibility of our attaining to truth, as distinguished from mere usefulness, is denied.

This pragmatist skepticism, this optimistic religion of a self-
sufficient humanity, has been substituted today, to a very considerable extent, in most of the Protestant communions, for the redemptive religion hitherto known as Christianity—that
redemptive religion with its doctrines of the awful transcendence
of God, the hopelessness of a mankind lost in sin, and the mysterious grace of God in the mighty redemptive acts of the coming

and death and resurrection of Jesus Christ. Many of the rank and file of the churches, many of the individual congregations, are genuinely Christian, but the central organizations of the churches have in many cases gradually discontinued their propagation of the Christian religion and have become agencies for the propagation of a vague type of religion to which Christianity from its very beginning was diametrically opposed.

So, in speaking about the responsibility of the church in the new age, I want it to be distinctly understood that I am not speaking about the responsibility of the existing Protestant church organizations (unless they can be reformed), but about the responsibility of a true Christian church. The present ecclesiastical organizations may have their uses in the world. There may be a need for such societies of general welfare as some of them have become; there may be a need for the political activities in which they are increasingly engaged: but such functions are certainly not at all the distinctive function of a real Christian church.

Even in the sphere of such worldly functions, I am inclined to think that there are agencies more worthy of your attention than these Protestant church organizations, or than, for example, such an organization as the Federal Council of the Churches of Christ in America. The trouble is that the gentlemen in control of these organizations are, though with the best and most honorable intentions in the world, in a hopelessly false position. The churches are for the most part creedal; it is on the basis of their creeds that they have in the past appealed, and that to some extent they still appeal, for support; yet the central organizations of the churches have quietly pushed the creeds into the background and have devoted themselves to other activities and a different propaganda. Perhaps in doing so they have accomplished good here and there in a worldly sort of way. But, in general, the false position in which they stand has militated against their highest usefulness. Equivocation, the double use of traditional terminology, subscription to solemn creedal statements in a sense different from the sense originally intended in those statements—these things give a man a poor platform upon which to stand, no matter what it is that he proposes, upon that platform, to do.

But if the existing Protestant church organizations, with some notable exceptions, must be radically reformed before they can be

regarded as truly Christian, what, as distinguished from these organizations, is the function of a true Christian church?

In the first place, a true Christian church, now as always, will
be radically doctrinal. It will never use the shibboleths of a pragmatist skepticism. It will never say that doctrine is the expression
of experience; it will never confuse the useful with the true, but
will place truth at the basis of all its striving and all its life. Into the
welter of changing human opinion, into the modern despair with
regard to any knowledge of the meaning of life, it will come with
a clear and imperious message. That message it will find in the Bible, which it will hold to contain not a record of man's religious
experience but a record of a revelation from God.

In the second place, a true Christian church will be radically
intolerant. At that point, however, a word of explanation is in
place. The intolerance of the church, in the sense in which I am
speaking of it, does not involve any interference with liberty, on
the contrary, it means the preservation of liberty. One of the most
important elements in civil and religious liberty is the right of voluntary association—the right of citizens to band themselves together for any lawful purpose whatever, whether that purpose does
or does not commend itself to the generality of their fellow men.
Now, a church is a voluntary association. No one is compelled to
be a member of it; no one is compelled to be one of its accredited
representatives. It is, therefore, no interference with liberty for a
church to insist that those who do choose to be its accredited representatives shall not use the vantage ground of such a position to
attack that for which the church exists.

It would, indeed, be an interference with liberty for a church,
through the ballot box or otherwise, to use the power of the state
to compel men to assent to the church's creed or conform to the
church's program. To that kind of intolerance I am opposed with
all my might and main. I am also opposed to church union for
somewhat similar reasons, as well as for other reasons still more important. I am opposed to the depressing dream of one monopolistic
church organization, placing the whole Protestant world under
one set of committees and boards. If that dream were ever realized,
it would be an intolerable tyranny. Certainly it would mean the
death of any true Christian unity. I trust that the efforts of the

church-unionists may be defeated, like the efforts of the opponents of liberty in other fields.

But when I say that a true Christian church is radically intolerant, I mean simply that the church must maintain the high exclusiveness and universality of its message. It presents the gospel of Jesus Christ not merely as one way of salvation, but as the only way. It cannot make common cause with other faiths. It cannot agree not to proselytize. Its appeal is universal and admits of no exceptions. All are lost in sin; none may be saved except by the way set forth in the gospel. Therein lies the offense of the Christian religion, but therein lies also its glory and its power. A Christianity tolerant of other religions is just no Christianity at all.

In the third place, a true Christian church will be radically ethical. It will not be ethical in the sense that it will cherish any hope in an appeal to the human will; it will not be ethical in the sense that it will regard itself as perfect, even when its members have been redeemed by the grace of God. But it will be ethical in the sense that it will cherish the hope of true goodness in the other world, and that even here and now it will exhibit the beginnings of a new life which is the gift of God.

That new life will express itself in love. Love will overflow, without questions, without calculation, to all men whether they be Christians or not; but it will be far too intense a passion ever to be satisfied with a mere philanthropy. It will offer men simple benefits; it will never pass coldly by on the other side when a man is in bodily need. But it will never be content to satisfy men's bodily needs; it will never seek to make men content with creature comforts or with the coldness of a vague natural religion. Rather will it seek to bring all men everywhere, without exception, high and low, rich and poor, learned and ignorant, compatriot and alien, into the full warmth and joy of the household of faith.

There are certain things which you cannot expect from such a true Christian church. In the first place, you cannot expect from it any cooperation with non-Christian religion or with a non-Christian program of ethical culture. There are those who tell us that the Bible ought to be put into the public schools, and that the public schools should seek to build character by showing the children that honesty is the best policy and that good Americans do not lie nor steal. With such programs a true Christian church will have

nothing to do. The Bible, it will hold, is made to say the direct opposite of what it means if any hope is held out to mankind from its
ethical portions apart from its great redemptive center and core;
and character building on the basis of human experience may be
character destruction; it is the very antithesis of that view of sin
which is at the foundation of all Christian convictions and all
Christian life.

There is no such thing, a true Christian church will insist, as a
universally valid fund of religious principles upon which particular
religions, including the Christian religion, may build; "religion" in
that vague sense is not only inadequate but false; and a morality
based upon human experience instead of upon the law of God is
no true morality. Against such programs of religious education and
character building, a true Christian church will seek from the state
liberty for all parents everywhere to bring up their children in accordance with the dictates of their conscience, will bring up its
own children in accordance with the Word of God, and will try to
persuade all other parents, becoming Christians, to bring up their
children in that same Christian way.

In the second place, you cannot expect from a true Christian
church any official pronouncements upon the political or social
questions of the day, and you cannot expect cooperation with the
state in anything involving the use of force. Important are the
functions of the police, and members of the church, either individ-
ually or in such special associations as they may choose to form,
should aid the police in every lawful way in the exercise of those
functions. But the function of the church in its corporate capacity
is of an entirely different kind. Its weapons against evil are spiritual, not carnal; and by becoming a political lobby, through the advocacy of political measures whether good or bad, the church is
turning aside from its proper mission, which is to bring to bear
upon human hearts the solemn and imperious, yet also sweet and
gracious, appeal of the gospel of Christ.

Such things you cannot expect from a true Christian church.
But there are other things which you may expect. If you are dissatisfied with a relative goodness, which is no goodness at all; if you
are conscious of your sin and if you hunger and thirst after righteousness; if you are dissatisfied with the world and are seeking the
living God, then turn to the Church of Jesus Christ. That church

is not always easy to distinguish today. It does not always present itself to you in powerful organizations; it is often hidden away here and there, in individual congregations resisting the central ecclesiastical mechanism; it is found in groups, large or small, of those who have been redeemed from sin and are citizens of a heavenly kingdom. But wherever it is found, you must turn to that true Church of Jesus Christ for a message from God. The message will not be enforced by human authority or by the pomp of numbers. Yet some of you may hear it. If you do hear it and heed it, you will possess riches greater than the riches of all the world.

Do you think that if you heed the message you will be less successful students of political and social science; do you think that by becoming citizens of another world you will become less fitted to solve this world's problems; do you think that acceptance of the Christian message will hinder political or social advance? No, my friends. I will present to you a strange paradox but an assured truth—this world's problems can never be solved by those who make this world the object of their desires. This world cannot ultimately be bettered if you think that this world is all. To move the world you must have a place to stand.

This, then, is the answer that I give to the question before us. The responsibility of the church in the new age is the same as its responsibility in every age. It is to testify that this world is lost in sin; that the span of human life—nay, all the length of human history—is an infinitesimal island in the awful depths of eternity; that there is a mysterious, holy, living God, Creator of all, Upholder of all, infinitely beyond all; that He has revealed Himself to us in His Word and offered us communion with Himself through Jesus Christ the Lord; that there is no other salvation, for individuals or for nations, save this, but that this salvation is full and free, and that whosoever possesses it has for himself and for all others to whom he may be the instrument of bringing it a treasure compared with which all the kingdoms of the earth—nay, all the wonders of the starry heavens—are as the dust of the street.

An unpopular message it is—an impractical message, we are told. But it is the message of the Christian church. Neglect it, and you will have destruction; heed it, and you will have life.

Sources for the Study of the Orthodox Presbyterian Church

Video

The Orthodox Presbyterian Church (1993), a fifty-five minute production on the OPC's history available from the Committee on Christian Education, 607 North Easton Road, Building E, Box P, Willow Grove, PA 19090.

Books and Articles

*Robert K. Churchill. *Lest We Forget: A Personal Reflection on the Formation of the Orthodox Presbyterian Church*. Philadelphia: Committee for the Historian, 1986.

*Charles G. Dennison. *The History of the Orthodox Presbyterian Church: An Annotated Bibliography*. rev. ed. Pittsburgh: Committee for the Historian, 1994.

Charles G. Dennison. "Machen, Culture and the Church." *Banner of Truth* (July 1987): 20–27, 32.

*Charles G. Dennison, ed. *The Orthodox Presbyterian Church: 1936–1986*. Philadelphia: Committee for the Historian, 1986.

*Charles G. Dennison and Richard C. Gamble, eds. *Pressing Toward the Mark: Essays Commemorating Fifty Years of the Orthodox Presbyterian Church*. Philadelphia: Committee for the Historian, 1986.

Charles G. Dennison. "Tragedy, Hope, and Ambivalence: The History of the Orthodox Presbyterian Church, 1936–1962." *Mid-America Journal of Theology.* Three articles beginning with 2 (1992).

Clarence W. Duff. *God's Higher Ways: The Birth of a Church.* Nutley: Presbyterian and Reformed, 1977.

D. G. Hart. *Defending the Faith: J. Gresham Machen and the Crisis of Conservative Protestantism in Modern America.* Grand Rapids: Baker, 1995.

D. G. Hart. "The Legacy of J. Gresham Machen and the Identity of the Orthodox Presbyterian Church." *Westminster Theological Journal* 53 (1991): 209–225.

Bruce F. Hunt. *For a Testimony.* London: Banner of Truth, 1966.

J. Gresham Machen. *Christianity and Liberalism.* New York: Macmillan, 1923 (currently available from Eerdmans).

Robert S. Marsden, ed. *The First Ten Years.* Philadelphia: Committee on Home Missions and Church Extension, 1946.

Mark Noll. "The Pea Beneath the Mattress—Orthodox Presbyterians in America." *The Reformed Journal* 36 (October 1986): 11–16.

*Edwin H. Rian. *The Presbyterian Conflict.* rev. ed. Philadelphia: Committee for the Historian, 1992.

Ned B. Stonehouse. *J. Gresham Machen: A Biographical Memoir.* Grand Rapids: Eerdmans, 1954 (currently available from Banner of Truth).

*William White, Jr. *Van Til: Defender of the Faith.* Nashville: Thomas Nelson, 1979.

*Available from the Committee for the Historian, Box 48, Coraopolis, PA 15108.

Index